D0934385

CHECKS AND BALANCES
IN THE U.S. GOVERNMENT

The Legislative Branch
Making Laws

EDITED BY BRIAN DUIGNAN AND CAROLYN DECARLO

Britannica
Educational Publishing

IN ASSOCIATION WITH

ROSEN
EDUCATIONAL SERVICES

Published in 2019 by Britannica Educational Publishing (a trademark of Encyclopædia Britannica, Inc.) in association with The Rosen Publishing Group, Inc.
29 East 21st Street, New York, NY 10010

Distributed exclusively by Rosen Publishing.
To see additional Britannica Educational Publishing titles, go to rosenpublishing.com.

Britannica Educational Publishing
J.E. Luebering: Executive Director, Core Editorial
Andrea R. Field: Managing Editor, Compton's by Britannica

Rosen Publishing
Carolyn DeCarlo: Editor
Nelson Sá: Art Director
Brian Garvey: Series Designer/Book Layout
Cindy Reiman: Photography Manager
Bruce Donnola: Photo Researcher

Library of Congress Cataloging-in-Publication Data

Names: Duignan, Brian, editor. | DeCarlo, Carolyn, editor.
Title: The legislative branch : making laws / edited by Brian Duignan and Carolyn DeCarlo.
Description: New York : Britannica Educational Publishing, in Association with Rosen Educational Services, 2019. | Series: Checks and balances in the U.S. government | Includes bibliographical references and index. | Audience: Grades 7-12.
Identifiers: LCCN 2017059716| ISBN 9781538301708 (library bound : alk. paper)
| ISBN 9781538301715 (pbk. : alk. paper)
Subjects: LCSH: United States. Congress—Juvenile literature. | Legislative power—United States—Juvenile literature. | Legislation—United States—Juvenile literature.
Classification: LCC JK1025 .L44 2019 | DDC 328.73—dc23
LC record available at https://lccn.loc.gov/2017059716

Manufactured in the United States of America

Photo credits: Cover, p. 1 Alex Wong/Getty Images (Congress), Lightspring/Shutterstock.com (scale), © iStockphoto.com/arsenisspyros (capitol); p. 5 © MedioImages/Getty Images; p. 6 Riverside County Registrar/KRT/Newscom; p. 9 © Library of Congress, Washington, D.C. (digital file no. 3g07216); p. 16 © Library of Congress, Washington, D.C. (LC-USZC4-10297); p. 18 Win McNamee/Getty Images; p. 20 Karl Gehring/Denver Post/Getty Images; p. 22 © Library of Congress, Washington, D.C. (neg. no. lc-usz61-269); pp. 26, 95 Bettmann/Getty Images; p. 29 Visions of America/Universal Images Group/Getty Images; pp. 30, 77, 107 © Encyclopaedia Britannica; p. 32 © Architect of the Capitol; p. 37 The Washington Post/Getty Images; p. 38 © AP Images; p. 41 © Lawrence Jackson – Official White House Photo; pp. 45, 89 Hulton Archive/Getty Images; p. 48 © Harris & Ewing Collection/Library of Congress, Washington, D.C. (LC-DIG-hec-22504); p. 51 © U.S. Senate Photo Studio; p. 56 © Dave Newman/Fotolia; p. 60 © Mike Criss; p. 64 © Chuck Kennedy - Official White House Photo; p. 67 © Peter Souza - Official White House Photo; pp. 75, 86, 103 © Library of Congress, Washington, D.C.; p. 91 MPI/Archive Photos/Getty Images; p. 105 © Tim Ross; p. 111 Library of Congress Prints and Photographs Division Washington, D.C. 20540 USA.

CONTENTS

The characteristic function of all legislatures is the making of law. In most political systems, however, legislatures also have other tasks, such as selecting and criticizing the government, supervising administration, appropriating funds, ratifying treaties, impeaching officials of the executive and judicial branches of government, accepting or refusing executive nominations, determining election procedures, and conducting public hearings on petitions. Legislatures, then, are not simply lawmaking bodies. Neither do they monopolize the function of making law. In most systems, the executive has a power of veto over legislation, and, even where this is lacking, the executive may exercise original or delegated powers of legislation. Judges, also, often share in the lawmaking process through the interpretation and application of statutes or, as in the U.S. system, by means of judicial review of legislation. Similarly, administrative officials exercise quasi-legislative powers in making rules and deciding cases that come before administrative tribunals.

A legislature may be unicameral, with one chamber, or bicameral, with two chambers. Unicameral legislatures are typical in small countries with unitary systems of government—i.e., systems in which local or regional governments may exist but in which the central government retains ultimate sovereignty. Federal states, in which the central government shares sovereignty with local or regional governments, usually have bicameral legislatures, with one house representing the main territorial subdivisions. The United States is a classic example of a federal system with a bicameral legislation: the U.S. Congress consists of a House of Representatives, whose members are elected from single-member districts of approximately

The west front of the U.S. Capitol building, Washington, D.C., where both houses of the U.S. Congress convene.

equal population, and a Senate, consisting of two persons from each state elected by the voters of that state. The fact that all states are represented equally in the Senate regardless of their size reflects the federal character of the American union.

A unitary system of government does not necessarily imply unicameralism. In fact, the legislatures of most countries with unitary systems are bicameral, though one chamber is usually more powerful than the other. The United Kingdom, for example, has a unitary system with a bicameral legislature, which consists of the House of Lords and the House of Commons. Although in the United States all fifty states except Nebraska have bicameral legislatures, their governmental systems are unitary. In the forty-nine U.S. states with bicameral legislatures, the two houses have equal legislative authority, but the so-called upper houses— usually called senates— have the special function of confirming the governors' appointments. The procedures of the U.S. House of Representatives, which derive from

A woman with her child uses an electronic voting system to exercise her right to vote in California.

a manual of procedure written by Thomas Jefferson, are among the most elaborate of parliamentary rules.

Voting procedures range from state to state; a popular method is the electronic voting methods employed in the California legislature and in some other states. Another point of difference among legislatures concerns their presiding officers. These are sometimes officials who stand above party and exercise a neutral function as parliamentary umpires; sometimes they are the leaders of the majority party and, like the speaker of the U.S. House of Representatives, major political figures; and sometimes they are officials who, like the vice president of the United States in his role as presiding officer of the Senate, exercise a vote to break ties and otherwise perform mainly ceremonial functions.

Likewise, legislative parties are of various types and play a number of roles or functions. In the U.S. House of Representatives, for example, the party is responsible for assigning members to all standing committees; the party leadership fills the major parliamentary offices, and the party membership on committees reflects the proportion of seats held by the party in the House as a whole. The congressional party, however, is not disciplined to the degree found in British and some other European legislative parties, and there are relatively few "party line" votes in which all the members of one party vote against all the members of the other party.

CHAPTER ONE

POWERS AND FUNCTIONS OF THE U.S. CONGRESS

The U.S. Congress, the legislative branch of the American federal system, was established under the Constitution of 1789 and is separated structurally from the executive and judicial branches of government. As noted previously, it consists of two houses: the Senate, in which each state, regardless of its size, is represented by two senators, and the House of Representatives, to which members are elected on the basis of population. Among the express powers of Congress as defined in the Constitution are the power to lay and collect taxes, borrow money on the credit of the United States, regulate commerce, coin money, declare war, raise and support armies, and make all laws necessary for the execution of its powers.

THE CONTINENTAL AND CONFEDERATION CONGRESSES

The Congress established in 1789 was the successor of the Continental Congress, which met in 1774 and 1775–81, and of the Confederation Congress, which met under the Articles of Confederation (1781–89), the first constitution of the United States. The First Continental Congress was convened in Philadelphia in 1774 in response to the British Parliament's passage of the Intolerable (Coercive) Acts, which were intended as punishment for the Boston Tea Party and other acts of colonial defiance. Fifty-six deputies in a single chamber represented all the colonies except Georgia. Peyton Randolph of Virginia was unanimously elected president, thus establishing usage of that term as well as "Congress." Other delegates included Patrick Henry, George Washington, John and Samuel Adams, and John Jay. Meeting in secret session, the body adopted a declaration of personal rights, including life, liberty,

Leaders of the Continental Congress (*left to right*): John Adams, Gouverneur Morris, Alexander Hamilton, and Thomas Jefferson.

property, assembly, and trial by jury, and denounced taxation without representation and the maintenance of the British army in the colonies without their consent.

Before the Second Continental Congress assembled in Philadelphia in 1775, hostilities had already broken out between Americans and British troops at Lexington and Concord, Massachusetts. New members of the Second Congress included Benjamin Franklin and Thomas Jefferson. John Hancock and John Jay were among those who served as president. The Congress "adopted" the New England military forces that had converged upon Boston and appointed Washington commander in chief of the American army. It also acted as the provisional government of the 13 colony-states, issuing and borrowing money, establishing a postal service, and creating a navy. On July 2, 1776, with New York abstaining, the Congress "unanimously" resolved that "these United Colonies are, and of right ought to be, free and independent states." Two days later, it solemnly approved this Declaration of Independence. The Congress also prepared the Articles

A PROPOSAL FOR A CONTINENTAL CONGRESS

Early in May 1774 the Boston Committee of Correspondence sent a circular letter throughout the colonies urging a stoppage of trade with Britain.

In New York, a committee of fifty-one, dominated by merchants, drafted a reply on May 23. While this committee had no desire to halt trade, it was determined to maintain control of the anti-British sentiments of the populace. The reply, therefore, sympathized with Boston's situation but implied that only a Continental Congress could suitably handle the matter:

The alarming measures of the British Parliament relative to your ancient and respectable town, which has so long been the seat of freedom, fill the inhabitants of this city with inexpressible concern. As a sister colony, suffering in defense of the rights of America, we consider your injuries as a common cause, to the redress of which it is equally our duty and our interest to contribute. But what ought to be done in a situation so truly critical, while it employs the anxious thoughts of every generous mind, is very hard to be determined.

Our citizens have thought it necessary to appoint a large committee, consisting of fifty-one persons, to correspond with our sister colonies on this and every other matter of public moment, and at ten o'clock this forenoon we were first assembled. Your letter, enclosing the vote of the town of Boston, and the letter of your Committee of Correspondence were immediately taken into consideration.

(CONTINUED ON THE NEXT PAGE)

(CONTINUED FROM THE PREVIOUS PAGE)

While we think you justly entitled to the thanks of your sister colonies for asking their advice on a case of such extensive consequences, we lament our inability to relieve your anxiety by a decisive opinion. The cause is general, and concerns a whole continent, who are equally interested with you and us; and we foresee that no remedy can be of avail unless it proceeds from the joint act and approbation of all; from a virtuous and spirited union which may be expected while the feeble efforts of a few will only be attended with mischief and disappointment to themselves and triumph to the adversaries of our liberty.

Upon these reasons we conclude that a congress of deputies from the colonies in general is of the utmost moment; that it ought to be assembled without delay, and some unanimous resolution formed in this fatal emergency, not only respecting your deplorable circumstances, but for the security of our common rights.

We have nothing to add, but that we sincerely condole with you in your unexampled distress, and to request your speedy opinion of the proposed congress, that if it should meet with your approbation, we may exert our utmost endeavors to carry it into execution.

of Confederation, which, after being sanctioned by all the states, became the first U.S. constitution in March 1781.

The Articles placed Congress on a constitutional basis, legalizing the powers it had exercised since 1775. This Confederation Congress continued to function until the new Congress, elected under the present Constitution, met in 1789.

THE CONGRESS OF 1789

The Constitutional Convention (1787) was called the Confederation Congress for the purpose of remedying certain defects in the Articles of Confederation. But the Virginia Plan, presented by the delegates from Virginia and often dubbed the large-state plan, went beyond revision and boldly proposed to introduce a new, national government in place of the existing confederation. The convention thus immediately faced the question of whether the United States was to be a country in the modern sense or would continue as a weak federation of autonomous and equal states represented in a single chamber, which was the principle embodied in the competing New Jersey Plan, presented by several small states (and hence has been referred to as the small-state plan). This decision was effectively made when a compromise plan for a bicameral legislature—one chamber with representation based on population and one with equal representation for all states—was approved in mid-June.

The Constitution, as it emerged after a summer of debate, embodied a much stronger principle of separation of powers than was generally to be found in the state constitutions. The chief executive was to be a single figure and was to be elected by an electoral college, meeting in the states. This followed much debate over the Virginia Plan's preference for legislative election of the executive. The principal control on the chief executive, or president, against violation of the Constitution was the threat of impeachment (a criminal proceeding instituted by a legislative body against a public official). The Virginia Plan's proposal that representation be proportional to population in both houses was severely modified by the retention of equal representation for each state in the Senate. The question of whether to count slaves in the population was abrasive; eventually, though, antislavery forces gave way to a compromise by which three-fifths of the slaves would be counted as population for purposes of representation and direct taxation. (For representation purposes, "Indians not taxed" were excluded.) Slave states would be perpetually overrepresented in national politics as a result; provision was also added for a law permitting the recapture of fugitive slaves.

At the time, political theory expected the legislature to be the most powerful branch of government. Thus, to balance the system, the executive was given a veto and a judicial system with powers of review was established. It was also implicit in the structure that the new federal judiciary would have power to veto any state laws that conflicted either with the Constitution or with federal statutes. States were forbidden to pass laws impairing obligations of contract—a measure aimed at encouraging capital—and the Congress could pass no ex post facto law (typically, a law that retroactively makes criminal an act that was not criminal when performed). But the Congress was endowed with the basic powers of a modern—and sovereign—government. The prospect of eventual enlargement of federal power appeared in the clause, giving the Congress powers to pass legislation "necessary and proper" for implementing the general purposes of the Constitution.

By June 1788 the Constitution had been ratified by nine states, as required by Article VII. After elections held late that year, the first Congress under the new Constitution convened in New York on March 4, 1789.

CONGRESS IS IN SESSION

Although the two chambers of Congress are separate, for the most part, they have an equal role in the enactment of legislation, and there are several aspects of the business of Congress that the Senate and the House of Representatives share and that require common action. Congress must assemble at least once a year and must agree on the date for convening and adjourning. The date for convening was set in the Constitution as the first Monday in

December. However, in the Twentieth Amendment to the Constitution, the date was changed to January 3. The date for adjournment is voted on by the House and the Senate. Congress must also convene in a joint session to count the electoral votes for the president and vice president. Although not required by the Constitution, joint sessions are also held when the president or some visiting dignitary addresses both houses.

Of common interest to both houses of Congress are also such matters as government printing, general accounting, and the congressional budget. Congress has established

President Woodrow Wilson delivers his War Message, asking for a declaration of war against Germany, to a joint session of Congress, 1917.

individual agencies to serve these specific interests. Other agencies, which are held directly responsible to Congress, include the Copyright Royalty Tribunal, the Botanic Garden, and the Library of Congress.

The term of Congress extends from each odd-numbered year to the next odd-numbered year. For its annual sessions, Congress developed the committee system to facilitate its consideration of the various items of business that arise. Each house of Congress has a number of standing (permanent) committees and select (special and temporary) committees. Together the two chambers of Congress form joint committees to consider subjects of common interest. Moreover, because no act of Congress is valid unless both houses approve an identical document, conference committees are formed to adjust disputed versions of legislation.

At the beginning of a session, the president delivers a State of the Union address, which describes in broad terms the legislative program that the president would like Congress to consider. Later, the president submits an annual budget message and the report on the economy prepared by the president's Council of Economic Advisors. Inasmuch as congressional committees require a period of time for preparing legislation before it is presented for general consideration, the legislative output of Congress may be rather small in the early weeks of a session. Legislation not enacted at the end of a session retains its status in the following session of the same two-year Congress.

RESTRAINTS ON CONGRESSIONAL POWER

In terms of legislation, the president may be considered a functioning part of the congressional process. The president is expected to keep Congress informed of the need for new legislation, and government departments and agencies are required to send Congress periodic reports of their activities. The president also submits certain types of treaties and nominations for the approval of the Senate. One of the most important legislative functions of the president, however, is that of signing or vetoing proposed legislation.

President Donald Trump addresses a joint session of Congress on February 28, 2017.

The president's veto may be overridden by a two-thirds vote of each chamber of Congress; nevertheless, the influence of the president's potential power may extend to the procedures of Congress. The possibility that a bill may be vetoed gives the president some influence in determining what legislation Congress will consider initially and what amendments will be acceptable. In addition to these legal and constitutional powers, the president has influence as the leader of a political party; party policy both in Congress and among the electorate may be molded by the president.

Although the U.S. Supreme Court has no direct relations with Congress, the Supreme Court's implied power to invalidate legislation that violates the Constitution is an even stronger restriction on the powers of Congress than the presidential veto. Supreme Court and federal court decisions on the constitutionality of legislation outline the constitutional framework within which Congress can act.

LOBBYING

Congress is also affected by representative interest groups, though they are not part of the formal structure of Congress. Lobbyists on behalf of interest groups play a significant role in testifying before congressional hearings and in mobilizing public opinion on select issues. Lobbyists may write letters or call public officials, launch public-relations campaigns to influence public opinion, or give substantial election campaign contributions to favoured legislators or executives. The persons who lobby in these ways may be full-time officials of a powerful trade or agricultural association or labour union, individual professional lobbyists with many clients who pay for their services, or ordinary citizens who take the time to state their hopes or grievances. Cities and states, consumer and environmental protection and other "public interest" groups, and various branches of the federal government also maintain staff lobbyists in the United States.

Many interest groups make use of political action committees (PACs) to solicit voluntary campaign contributions from individuals and then channel the resulting funds to candidates for elective offices in the federal government, primarily in the House of Representatives and the Senate. PACs rose to prominence after the Federal Election Campaign Act of 1971 set strict limits on the amount of money a particular corporation, union, or private individual could give to a candidate. By soliciting smaller contributions from a much larger number of

A lobbyist for locally owned convenience stores and gas stations in Colorado listens t testimony presented before the state finance committee at the state capitol.

individuals, PACs circumvent these limitations and manage to provide substantial funds for candidates.

As a result of the U.S. Supreme Court's decision in *Citizens United* v. *Federal Election Commission* (2010), corporations and unions, and later individuals, were eventually able to donate unlimited funds to independent PACs advocating on behalf of individual candidates or political parties. They could also donate anonymously and without limit to independent political advocacy groups that had declared themselves "social welfare" organizations in order to avoid donor-disclosure requirements. Such anonymously donated funds came to be known as "dark money."

ADDITIONAL FUNCTIONS OF CONGRESS

Many of the activities of Congress are not directly concerned with enacting laws, but the ability of Congress to enact law is often the sanction that makes its other actions effective. The general legal theory under which Congress operates is that legal authority is delegated to the president or executive departments and agencies and that the latter, in turn, are legally responsible for their actions. Congress may review any actions performed by a delegated authority; in some areas of delegated legislation—such as proposals for governmental reorganization—Congress must indicate approval of specific plans before they go into effect. Congress may also retain the right to terminate legislation by joint action of both houses.

Congress exercises general legal control over the employment of government personnel. Political control may also be exercised, particularly through the Senate's power to advise and consent to nominations. Neither the Senate nor the House of Representatives has any direct constitutional power to nominate or otherwise select executive or judicial personnel (although in the unusual event that the electoral college fails to select a president and vice president, the two houses, respectively, are expected to do so). Furthermore, Congress does not customarily remove officials. Congress, however, does have the power of impeachment. In such proceedings, the impeachment is made by the House of Representatives, and the case is tried before the Senate—a vote of two-thirds of the senators present is required for conviction.

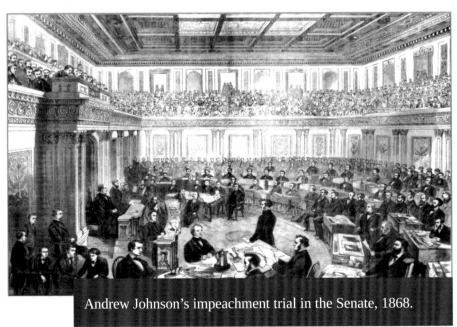

Andrew Johnson's impeachment trial in the Senate, 1868.

The power to levy and collect taxes and to appropriate funds allows Congress considerable authority in fiscal matters. Although the president has the initial responsibility for determining the proposed level of appropriations, once estimates for the next fiscal year are submitted to Congress, a single budget bill is not enacted, but rather a number of appropriation bills for various departments and agencies are passed during the first six or seven months of a session. In its nonlegislative capacity, Congress also has the power to initiate amendments to the Constitution, and it must determine whether the states should vote on a proposed amendment by state legislatures or by special state conventions. Finally, Congress has the right to investigate any subject that affects its powers. Congressional investigating committees may call witnesses and require them to produce information. These committees may also be given the power to charge with contempt of Congress persons who deliberately block the legislative process and to issue warrants for their arrest.

Since 1945 the activities and politics of the U.S. Congress have been reported in a group of periodicals called the *Congressional Quarterly (CQ)*, published in Washington, D.C. *CQ* comprises a Weekly Report with a Quarterly Index, an annual Almanac, and a news service. In addition, various special volumes and series are published from time to time, reviewing significant government activities and special problems. In addition to news media, *CQ*'s users include libraries, lobbyists, and many government congressional offices.

CHAPTER TWO

THE U.S. CAPITOL AND LIBRARY OF CONGRESS

The major buildings associated with the legislative branch of the federal government are the United States Capitol and the Library of Congress complex.

UNITED STATES CAPITOL

The Congress of the United States meets in the United States Capitol, one of the most familiar landmarks in Washington, D.C. It is situated on Capitol Hill at the eastern end of Pennsylvania Avenue. The Washington Monument and the Lincoln Memorial lie to the west, and the Supreme Court and the Library of Congress lie to the east. The Supreme Court held sessions in the Capitol until its own building was completed in 1935.

Pierre Charles L'Enfant, who had designed the basic plan of Washington, was also expected to design the Capitol. Claiming that the plan was "in his head," however, L'Enfant refused to submit drawings or work with local commissioners, and President George Washington was forced to dismiss him. A plan by William Thornton, a versatile physician with no formal architectural training, was eventually accepted, though it was submitted months after the closure of a design competition held in 1792. Thomas Jefferson, who was then secretary of state, was impressed with Thornton's design, writing that it, "so captivated the eyes and judgment of all as to leave no doubt... of its preference over all which have been produced.... It is simple, noble, beautiful, excellently distributed and moderate in size." The cornerstone was laid by Washington on September 18, 1793.

Because Thornton had no knowledge of building technology, the construction was initially supervised by the runner-up in the competition, Stephen Hallet. Hallet attempted to alter many of Thornton's plans and was quickly replaced, first by George Hadfield and later by James Hoban, the architect who designed the White House.

The north wing, containing the Senate chamber, was completed first, and Congress convened there in November 1800. The following year Jefferson became the first president to be inaugurated at the Capitol, a tradition that has been observed in all subsequent inaugurations. The remainder of the building was completed by Benjamin Latrobe, whom Jefferson appointed surveyor of public buildings in 1803. Latrobe followed Thornton's conception of the exterior closely but used his own designs for the interior. Perhaps Latrobe's best-known additions were the unique Corinthian-style columns, whose capitals depict

Thomas Jefferson ties his horse to a fencepost before walking into his presidential inauguration in the newly constructed Capitol building.

tobacco leaves (symbolizing the nation's wealth) and corn cobs (symbolizing the country's bounty).

The south wing, containing the chamber of the House of Representatives, was completed in 1807. During the War of 1812 the Capitol was looted and burned by British troops, though rain prevented the building's complete devastation. Latrobe began reconstruction in 1815 but resigned two years later. By 1827 his successor, the distin-

LATROBE, THE ARCHITECT

Benjamin Latrobe (1764–1820) was a British-born architect and civil engineer who established architecture in the United States. He was the most original proponent of the Greek Revival style in American building.

Latrobe immigrated in 1795 to the United States, where his first important work was the State Penitentiary in Richmond, Virginia. Latrobe then moved to Philadelphia and in 1798 received the commission for the Bank of Pennsylvania, whose Ionic porticoes inspired countless imitations; the building is now considered the first monument of the Greek Revival in America.

In Richmond, Latrobe had met Thomas Jefferson, who, in 1803, made him surveyor of the public buildings of the United States. Latrobe inherited the task of completing the U.S. Capitol in Washington, D.C. In the House of Representatives and the Senate chambers, he incorporated American floral motifs into the classical scheme. His Supreme Court Chamber in the Capitol has a notably original American classical interior.

Latrobe's most famous work is the Basilica of the Assumption of the Blessed Virgin Mary, the Roman Catholic cathedral in Baltimore (begun 1805), a severe, beautifully proportioned structure slightly marred by the onion-shaped domes added posthumously to the towers above the portico.

guished Boston architect Charles Bulfinch, had joined the two wings and built the first copper-sheathed dome, again adhering to Thornton's original design. In January 1832 the French historian Alexis de Tocqueville visited the Capitol and observed that it was "a magnificent palace," though he was less impressed with the sessions of Congress, writing that they were "frequently vague and perplexed" and that they seemed to "drag their slow length along rather than to advance towards a distinct object."

In order to provide more space for the increasing numbers of legislators from new states, in 1850 Congress approved a competition for a design to expand both wings of the Capitol. The winner, the Philadelphia architect Thomas Ustick Walter, finished the extension of the south wing in 1857 and the north wing in 1859. The new additions did not seem to alter the behaviour of the members, however. Aleksandr Lakier, a Russian visitor to the United States, wrote that everyone:

...wears a black frock-coat or tails and sits where he pleases. Had I not felt regret for the nice new furniture and carpet in the House of Representatives, I would not even have noticed the rude, but perhaps comfortable, position of the feet raised by a son of the plains above the head of his neighbor, and the nasty habit many Americans have of chewing tobacco.

The major architectural change to the Capitol during Walter's tenure was the replacement of the old Bulfinch dome with a 287-foot-high (87-metre) cast-iron dome, which Walter modeled after the dome of St. Peter's Basilica in Rome, designed by Michelangelo. At the onset of the American Civil War, the dome remained unfinished, surrounded by scaffolding and cranes. In 1861 the Capitol was used temporarily to bivouac federal soldiers who had been hastily dispatched to protect Washington from an attack by the Confederacy. These soldiers set up camp in the House and Senate chambers and in the unfinished rotunda, occupying their free time by holding mock sessions of Congress and freely helping themselves to franked stationery. At the insistence of President Abraham Lincoln, work on the dome continued, despite the war, as an important symbol of national unity.

On December 2, 1863, Freedom, a bronze statue 19.5 feet (6 meters) high by Thomas Crawford, was installed on top of the dome's crowning cupola. Crawford's first drawings in the 1850s had adorned the statue

A replica of the bronze *Statue of Freedom* by Thomas Crawford, which is the crowning feature on the dome of the U.S. Capitol.

with a liberty cap—the symbol of freed slaves—but after objections from Jefferson Davis, then the secretary of war and later the president of the Confederacy, the cap was replaced with a Roman helmet. (According to records that surfaced in 2000, the workers who cast the statue, as well as the worker who devised the method of raising it, were slaves.) Constantino Brumidi's allegorical fresco *Apotheosis of Washington* (1865), which depicts gods and goddesses intermingled with George Washington and other American heroes, adorns the ceiling's dome. In 1864 Congress established what would later be called National Statuary Hall, where statues of two prominent figures from each

President John F. Kennedy's body is carried by pallbearers into the U.S. Capitol Rotunda on November 24, 1963.

state were to be displayed. (All the statues were to be displayed in National Statuary Hall, the original chamber of the House of Representatives; but by the 1930s engineers found that the weight of the many marble statues exceeded the floor's load-bearing capacity, thereby threatening its structure, and some statues were moved elsewhere.) After his assassination in April 1865, Lincoln became the first person to lie in state in the newly finished rotunda, an honour since bestowed on some thirty people.

With the exception of various modernizations, including the installation of central heating, electricity, and elevators, no significant architectural alterations or additions were made until 1959–60, when the east front was extended 32.5 feet (10 metres) under the supervision of J. George Stewart. In December 2008, the 580,000-square-foot (53,884-square-metre) Capitol Visitor Center opened. Designed as an underground extension of the Capitol, it features exhibits about the building and Congress. The centre also provides shelter to visitors who previously had to wait in lines outdoors. Not including the Capitol Visitor Center, the building contains about 540 rooms and stands in a 131-acre (53-hectare) park.

LIBRARY OF CONGRESS

The Library of Congress is the de facto national library of the United States and the largest library in the world. In 2016 it had some 164 million items, and its collection is growing at a rate of about 2 million items a year. The Library of Congress serves members, committees, and staff of the Congress, other government agencies, libraries throughout the country and the world, and the scholars, researchers, artists, and scientists who use its resources. It is the national centre for library service to the blind and physically handicapped, and it offers many concerts, lectures, and exhibitions for the general public. Those outside the Washington, D.C., area have access to the library's growing electronic resources through the Library of Congress website.

The library was founded in 1800 with $5,000 appropriated by the Congress when the U.S. capital moved

The facade of the Library of Congress's Jefferson Building in Washington, D.C., which was designed by the architectural firm of Smithmeyer and Pelz and completed in 1897.

from Philadelphia, Pennsylvania, to Washington, D.C. It was housed within the new Capitol building, where it remained for nearly a century. However, on August 24, 1814, during the War of 1812, the library's original collection of 3,000 volumes was destroyed when the British burned the Capitol as well as the White House. To rebuild the library's collection, Congress, on January 30, 1815, approved the purchase of former president Thomas Jefferson's personal library of 6,487 books for $23,950. On Christmas Eve 1851, another fire destroyed two-thirds of the collection. Many of the volumes have since been replaced.

Librarian of Congress Ainsworth Rand Spofford (1864–97) was the first to propose that the library be moved to a dedicated building. He also was instrumental in establishing the copyright law of 1870, which placed the Copyright Office in the Library of Congress and required anyone seeking a copyright to provide two copies of the work—books, pamphlets, maps, photographs, music, and prints—to the library.

Largely as a result of Spofford's vision, the library's burgeoning collection outgrew its space in the Capitol. In the early 21st century the Library of Congress complex on Capitol Hill included three buildings containing twenty-one public reading rooms. The Thomas Jefferson Building (originally called the Congressional Library, or Main Building) houses the Main Reading Room. Designed in Italian Renaissance style, it was completed in 1897 and magnificently restored 100 years later. The John Adams Building, completed in 1939, received its current name in 1980 to honour the president who in 1800 signed the act of Congress establishing the library. The Adams Building was built in Art Deco style and

DIGITAL MILLENNIUM COPYRIGHT ACT (1998)

The Digital Millennium Copyright Act was designed to adapt copyright laws to the rise of the Internet in the 1990s. Traditionally, copyright laws focused on published material, but the Internet made possible the electronic reproduction of virtually any document. The inadequacy of existing laws particularly alarmed businesses that needed copyright protection, such as book publishers, music recording companies, software publishers, and filmmakers. In response to these concerns, Congress passed the Digital Millennium Copyright Act in 1998. The act, among other provisions, banned the use of software that circumvented copyright protections in computer programs. Although many hailed the act as a wise step in protecting fundamental copyrights, some critics charged that it suppressed free speech and unfairly limited the freedom of computer scientists and researchers. Others warned that the act would ultimately backfire, claiming that it would deter research to study flaws in computer security programs.

faced with white Georgia marble. The James Madison Memorial Building, modern in style, was dedicated in 1980. (That same year the Main Building was designated the Thomas Jefferson Building.) The Madison Building more than doubled the library's available Capitol Hill space. The continued growth of the collection in a wide variety of formats during the 1980s and 1990s necessitated the off-site relocation of some materials to storage facilities in Fort Meade, Maryland, and to the Packard Campus of the National Audio-Visual Conservation Center in Culpeper, Virginia.

The vast majority of works in the library's collections are received through the copyright deposit process mentioned above. Materials are also acquired through gifts, purchases, and donations from private sources and other government agencies (state, local, and federal), the library's Cataloging in Publication program (a prepublication arrangement with publishers), and exchanges with libraries in the United States and abroad. Those items that are not selected for the library's collections or exchange programs are offered free to other federal agencies, educational institutions, public libraries, or nonprofit, tax-exempt organizations.

The library's collections include more than 32 million cataloged books and other print materials, more than 63 million manuscripts, 5.3 million maps, 5.6 million pieces of sheet music, more than 3 million audio materials, and more than 14 million visual materials (comprising more than 12.5 million photographs and 1 million moving images).

Approximately half of the library's book and serial collections are in languages other than English. Some 470 languages are represented. Particularly noteworthy are the library's preeminent collections in Arabic, Spanish, and Portuguese; the largest collections in many Slavic and Asian languages outside those geographic areas; the world's largest law library; and the largest rare-book collection in North America (some 750,000 volumes), including the most comprehensive collection of 15th-century books in the Western Hemisphere. The Manuscript Division holds the papers of twenty-three U.S. presidents, along with those of many other high-ranking government officials, of inventors such as Alexander Graham Bell and the Wright brothers, of social reformers such as Susan B. Anthony and Frederick Douglass, and of cultural figures such as Walt Whitman, Irving Berlin, and Martha Graham.

The Library of Congress provides direct research assistance to the U.S. Congress through the Congressional Research Service (originally the Legislative Reference Service), which was founded in 1914. Established in 1832, the Law Library provides Congress with comprehensive research on foreign, comparative, international, and U.S. law, drawing upon its collection of some 2.9 million volumes.

The Library of Congress is supported by direct appropriations from the Congress—as well as gifts and private donations—and has been governed since 1800 by the Joint Committee on the Library of Congress. Established in 1990, the James Madison Council—the library's first private-sector advisory group—has supported the acquisition of hundreds of collection items (such as the 1507 map by the German cartographer Martin Waldseemüller that first used the word "America") and initiatives such as the annual National Book Festival (launched in 2001). The council's first chairman, John W. Kluge, also endowed a major scholarly centre and a $1 million prize for lifetime achievement in the humanities.

In addition to the Kluge Prize, the library sponsors many privately endowed honours and awards recognizing creativity and achievement in the humanities. These include the poet laureate position, the Living Legend

The National Book Festival is held annually on the National Mall in Washington, D.C.

medal, the Gershwin Prize for Popular Song, and the National Ambassador for Young People's Literature, through which the library honours those who have advanced and embodied the ideals of individual creativity with conviction, dedication, scholarship, and exuberance.

In 1994 the Library of Congress launched the National Digital Library Program (NDLP), making high-quality electronic versions of American historical material from the library's special collections freely available on the Internet. By the end of the library's

U.S. poet laureate for 2017–18 Tracy K. Smith won the Pulitzer Prize in 2012 for he collection *Life on Mars*.

bicentennial year in 2000, more than five million items (manuscripts, films, sound recordings, and photographs) had been mounted on the library's American Memory Web site, which continued to expand rapidly. Also accessible on the website were the library's exhibitions, bibliographic databases (online public access catalog), a comprehensive legislative information system known as THOMAS, copyright information, and a Global Gateway website for the library's international collections and collaborative digital libraries built with international partners.

Inspired by the success of the Global Gateway site, in 2005 Librarian of Congress James H. Billington proposed a project called the World Digital Library. Its goal was to make available to anyone with access to the Internet digitized texts and images of "unique and rare materials from libraries and other cultural institutions around the world." It was designed to be searchable in seven languages—Arabic, Chinese, English, French, Russian, and Spanish (official languages of the United Nations), as well as Portuguese. In 2007 the Library of Congress and UNESCO signed an agreement to build a World Digital Library website, which was launched in 2009 with approximately 1,200 digitized exhibits, including books, maps, and paintings; in 2017 the library had over 17,000 searchable items. The library is also leading a collaborative effort mandated in 2000 by the Congress to preserve the country's digital assets.

CHAPTER THREE

THE HOUSE AND THE SENATE

The House of Representatives is sometimes referred to as the "lower" house of Congress, in contrast to the Senate, which is the "upper" house. These terms, however, do not appear in the Constitution, and they are misleading in their suggestion that the legislative powers of the Senate are greater than those of the House. In fact, the House and the Senate share equal responsibility for lawmaking.

THE HOUSE OF REPRESENTATIVES

As conceived by the framers of the Constitution, the House was designed to represent the popular will, and its members were to be directly elected by the people. In contrast, members of the Senate were appointed by the states until the ratification of the Seventeenth Amendment (1913), which mandated the direct election of senators.

The constitutional requirements for eligibility for membership in the House of Representatives are a

Chamber of the U.S. House of Representatives, Washington, D.C.

minimum age of 25 years, U.S. citizenship for at least seven years, and residency in the state from which the member is elected (a member need not reside in the constituency that he or she represents).

Each state is guaranteed at least one member of the House of Representatives. The allocation of seats is based on the population within the states, and membership is reapportioned every ten years following the decennial census. House members are elected for two-year terms from single-member districts of approximately equal population.

HOUSE ORGANIZATION

In order to ensure that the populations of different districts remain approximately equal, legislative apportionment sometimes involves the redrawing of electoral districts or the creation of new ones. The authority to alter apportionment can be an important tool in maintaining the power of the incumbent political party. Constituencies can be defined, for example, in a way that concentrates the power of the opposition into relatively few districts and gives the ruling party narrow majorities in a large number of

GERRYMANDERING

The term "gerrymandering" is derived from the name of Governor Elbridge Gerry of Massachusetts, whose administration enacted a law in 1812 defining new state senatorial districts. The law consolidated the Federalist Party vote in a few districts and thus gave disproportionate representation to Democratic-Republicans. A satirical cartoon by Elkanah Tisdale appeared in the *Boston Gazette*; it graphically transformed the districts into a fabulous animal, "The Gerrymander," fixing the term in the popular imagination. Gerrymandering thus came to mean the drawing of electoral-district boundaries in a way that gives one party an unfair advantage over others.

Gerrymandering has been condemned because it violates two basic tenets of electoral apportionment—compactness and equality of size of constituencies. A U.S. Supreme Court ruling of 1964 stated that districts should be drawn to reflect substantial equality of population. However, using studies of regional voting behaviour, the majority parties in certain state legislatures continue to set district boundaries along partisan lines without regard for local boundaries or even contiguity. For example, in some states, representatives from rural and small town districts seek to limit the representation of more densely populated urban centres.

Sometimes gerrymandering is defended as the only means of securing any representation for minority groups. It is argued that violating local boundaries in drawing districts is preferable to denying a politically cohesive group any voice in state government.

During the last two decades of the 20th century, some state legislatures in the United States undertook what amounted to racial gerrymandering to preserve the integrity and power of special-interest blocs of voters in large cities and other regions and to increase minority representation. However, the Supreme Court subsequently invalidated several racially gerrymandered majority-minority congressional districts and ruled that race could not be the determining factor in the drawing of constituency boundaries.

districts; the incumbent party is thereby awarded a disproportionately large share of seats. Using a different strategy, individual incumbents sometimes seek to influence
the apportionment process to give themselves districts
with no substantial opposition. The drawing of district
boundaries in a way that gives an unfair advantage to one
political party, a practice known as partisan or political
gerrymandering, is generally considered an abuse.

During the first Congress (1789–91), there were 59
members of the House of Representatives. By 1912 membership had reached 435. Two additional representatives
were added temporarily after the admission of Alaska
and Hawaii as states in 1959, but at the next legislative
apportionment membership returned to 435, the number
authorized by a law enacted in 1941.

The Constitution vests certain exclusive powers in the
House of Representatives, including the right to initiate
impeachment proceedings. Impeachment has rarely been
employed, however, largely because it is a lengthy, expensive, and politically charged process. The first president
to be impeached was Andrew Johnson (1865–69), who was
charged by the House of Representatives with attempting
to remove the secretary of war in violation of the Tenure
of Office Act; he was acquitted in the Senate by a single
vote. In 1974 the Judiciary Committee of the House of
Representatives voted three articles of impeachment
against President Richard M. Nixon in connection with
his role in the Watergate scandal, but he resigned before

impeachment proceedings in the full House could begin. In December 1998, the House of Representatives voted to impeach President Bill Clinton, charging him with perjury and obstruction of justice in investigations of his relationship with a White House intern, Monica Lewinsky. He was acquitted in the Senate.

A dominating element of House organization is the committee system, under which the membership is divided into specialized groups for purposes such as holding hearings, preparing bills for the consideration of the entire House, and regulating House procedure. A member of the majority party chairs each committee. Almost

Presided over by Chief Justice William Rehnquist, the U.S. Senate votes to acquit President Bill Clinton in 1999 following his impeachment two months earlier. A two-thirds majority was needed to remove the president from office.

all bills are first referred to a committee, and ordinarily the full House cannot act on a bill until the committee has "reported" it for floor action. There are approximately twenty standing (permanent) committees, organized mainly around major policy areas, each having staffs, budgets, and subcommittees. They may hold hearings on questions of public interest, propose legislation that has not been formally introduced as a bill or resolution, and conduct investigations. Important standing committees include those on appropriations, on ways and means (which handles matters related to finance), and on rules. There are also select and special committees, which are usually appointed for a specific project and for a limited period. The committees also play an important role in the control exercised by Congress over governmental agencies. Cabinet officers and other officials are frequently summoned before the committees to explain policy.

THE ANNUAL BUDGET

The House has the constitutional right to originate bills of taxation and spending. Since 1921, however, the annual budget of the United States has been proposed by the president and accepted or rejected, in whole or in part, by the House. It is prepared under his direct authority by the Office of Management and Budget (OMB). The process begins when the various departments and agencies prepare their appropriation requests, based on expenditures required under existing law and those estimated under new legislation to be proposed by the president. The OMB carefully scrutinizes these requests. In case of disagreement, cabinet officers negotiate directly with the president, who is ultimately responsible.

The budget is submitted in January and normally applies to appropriations for the fiscal year beginning July 1. These must normally be spent in the following two years. For some items, such as construction or procurement of military hardware, appropriations are made to cover expenditures for the whole construction period.

When the budget reaches the House of Representatives, it is distributed among the subcommittees of the Appropriations Committee. Each subcommittee is concerned with a particular organizational unit. There is virtually no consideration of the budget as a whole by the committee as a whole. Revenues fall under the jurisdiction of the Ways and Means Committee and are considered separately and possibly even at a different time from Appropriations.

The organization and character of the House of Representatives have evolved under the influence of political parties, which provide a means of controlling proceedings and mobilizing the necessary majorities. Party leaders, such as the speaker of the House and the majority and minority leaders, play a central role in the operations of the institution. However, party discipline (i.e., the tendency of all members of a political party to vote in the same way)

THE HOUSE UN-AMERICAN ACTIVITIES COMMITTEE

The House Un-American Activities Commit-tee (HUAC) was a standing committee of the U.S. House of Representatives, established in 1938 under Martin Dies, Jr., as chairman, that conducted investigations through the 1940s and 1950s into the alleged communist activities and associations of American citizens. Those in-vestigated included many artists and entertain-ers, including the writers Elia Kazan and Arthur Miller and the folk singer Pete Seeger. Richard

Martin Dies, Jr., 1937, first chairman of the House Un-American Activities Committee (HUAC).

Nixon was an active member of HUAC in the late 1940s. The committee's most celebrated case was perhaps that of Alger Hiss, a former State Department official accused of involvement in a Soviet espionage ring. HUAC's actions resulted in several contempt-of-Congress convictions and the "blacklisting" of many of those who refused to answer its questions. Highly controversial for its tactics, it was criticized for violating First Amendment rights. Its influence had waned by the 1960s. In 1969 it was renamed the Internal Security Committee, and in 1975 it was dissolved.

has not always been strong, owing to the fact that members, who must face reelection every two years, often vote in the interests of their districts rather than their political party when the two diverge.

Article I, section 6, paragraph 2 of the U.S. Constitution prohibits members of Congress from holding offices in the executive branch of government—a chief distinction between parliamentary and congressional forms of government:

No Senator or representative shall, during the time for which he was elected, be appointed to any civil office under the authority of the United States, which shall have been created, or the emoluments whereof shall have been increased during such time; and no person holding any office shall be a member of either House during his continuance in office.

After the census of 1920, Northeastern and Midwestern states held 270 House seats and the South and West held 169. Thereafter, the balance between the two regions gradually shifted: following the 2010 census, the Northeast and Midwest accounted for only 172 seats, compared with the South and West's 263. Most notably, the number of representatives from New York declined from 45 in the 1930s to only 27 in 2012, while the number from California increased from 11 to 53.

THE SENATE

The Senate, along with the House of Representatives, was established in 1789 under the Constitution of the United States. The Senate shares with the House responsibility for all lawmaking within the United States; for an act of Congress to be valid, both houses must approve an identical document. In addition, the Senate possesses certain important and exclusive powers, such as ratifying treaties and approving appointments to high federal offices.

HISTORY AND FUNCTIONS

The role of the Senate was conceived by the Founding Fathers as a check on the popularly elected House of

Chamber of the U.S. Senate, Washington, D.C.

Representatives. Thus each state, regardless of size or population, is equally represented. Further, until the Seventeenth Amendment of the Constitution (1913), election to the Senate was indirect, by the state legislatures. They are now elected directly by voters of each state.

Each state elects two senators for six-year terms, the terms of about one-third of the Senate membership expiring every two years. The constitutional provisions regarding qualifications for membership of the Senate specify a minimum age of 30, citizenship of the United States for nine years, and residence in the state from which elected.

The Senate is given important powers under the "advice and consent" provisions (Article II, section 2) of the Constitution:

> *[The President] shall have Power, by and with the Advice and Consent of the Senate, to make Treaties, provided two-thirds of the Senators present concur; and he shall nominate, and by and with the Advice and Consent of the Senate, shall appoint Ambassadors, other public Ministers and Consuls, Judges of the supreme Court, and all other Officers of the United States, whose Appointments are not herein otherwise provided for, and which shall be established by Law: but the Congress may by Law vest the Appointment of such inferior Officers, as they think proper, in the President alone, in the Courts of Law, or in the Heads of Departments.*

Ratification of treaties requires a two-thirds majority of all senators present and a simple majority for approval of important public appointments, such as those of cabinet members, ambassadors, and judges of the Supreme Court. The Senate also adjudicates impeachment proceedings initiated in the House of Representatives, a two-thirds majority being necessary for conviction.

As in the House of Representatives, political parties and the committee system dominate procedure and organization. Each party elects a leader, generally a senator of considerable influence in his own right, to coordinate Senate activities. The Senate leaders also play an important role in appointing members of their party to the Senate committees, which consider and process legislation and exercise general control over government agencies and departments. Sixteen standing committees are grouped mainly around major policy areas, each having staffs, budgets, and various subcommittees. Among important standing committees are those on appropriations, finance, government operations, and foreign relations. At "mark-up" sessions, which may be open or closed, the final language for a law is considered. Select and special committees are also created to make studies or to conduct investigations and report to the Senate—for example, the Select Committee on Ethics and the Special Committee on Aging.

THE RIGHT TO FILIBUSTER

The smaller membership of the Senate permits more extended debate than is common in the House of Representatives. Indeed, unlike the House of Representatives, in which speaking time is limited by rule, the Senate allows unlimited debate on a bill. Occasionally a minority of senators (sometimes even a single senator), using a parliamentary tactic known as a filibuster, will attempt to delay or prevent action on a bill by talking so long that the majority either grants concessions or withdraws the bill. To check a filibuster, three-fifths of the Senate membership must vote for cloture (or closure); if the bill under debate would change the Senate's standing rules, cloture may be invoked only on a vote of two-thirds of those present. The cloture motion itself is not debatable. Debate on the bill is then limited to an additional 30 hours.

In 1957 Senator Strom Thurmond of South Carolina talked for more than 24 hours, the longest individual filibuster on record, as part of an unsuccessful attempt by Southern senators to obstruct civil rights legislation.

Traditionally, senators could block a nominee to the Supreme Court through a filibuster, provided that less than three-fifths of the Senate supported cloture. When Justice Antonin Scalia died in February 2016, during the last year of Obama's presidency, Senate Republicans had refused to schedule a vote, or even to hold hearings, for the nominee selected by Obama as Scalia's replacement. Soon after his inauguration as president in January 2017, Donald Trump nominated Neil Gorsuch to the seat. Democratic senators mounted a filibuster of Gorsuch's nomination, which Republicans then defeated by eliminating the three-fifths requirement to end filibusters of Supreme Court nominees, replacing it with a simple majority, a change in Senate procedure so profound and far-reaching that both sides commonly referred to it as the "nuclear option."

There is a less-elaborate structure of party control in the Senate than there is in the House. The position taken by influential senators may be more significant than the position (if any) taken by the party.

CHAPTER FOUR

MAJOR LEGISLATION

In its more than 200-year existence, the U.S. Congress has passed countless laws and resolutions, some of which have been notable for the profound impact they achieved (or were intended to achieve) in a number of areas, including changes to the executive branch and federal government, civil rights and civil liberties, western territorial expansion, foreign relations, the administration of overseas territories, immigration, national security, property law, antitrust law, labour standards and worker's rights, and social welfare.

JUDICIARY ACT OF 1789

The Judiciary Act of 1789 established the organization of the U.S. federal court system, which had been sketched only in general terms in the U.S. Constitution. The act established a three-part judiciary—made up of district courts, circuit courts, and the Supreme Court—and outlined the structure and jurisdiction of each branch. The act was principally authored by senators Oliver Ellsworth

The U.S. Supreme Court Building, Washington, D.C., was designed by Cass Gilbert and completed in 1935.

and William Paterson and signed into law by President George Washington on September 24, 1789. The law's creators viewed it as a work in progress, but while it's been amended throughout the years, the basic outline it provided has remained intact.

The act divided the country into districts, with one court and one judge in each, along with attorneys responsible for civil and criminal actions in their districts. The act also created the office of attorney general of the United States; the attorney general, a member of the cabinet, is appointed by the president as head of the Department of Justice. Circuit courts—which make up the middle tier of

PENDLETON CIVIL SERVICE ACT (1883)

The Pendleton Civil Service Act was a landmark piece of legislation establishing the tradition and mechanism of permanent federal employment based on merit rather than on political party affiliation (the spoils system).

Widespread public demand for civil service reform was stirred after the Civil War by mounting incompetence, graft, corruption, and theft in federal departments and agencies. After President James A. Garfield was assassinated in 1881, civil service reform became a leading issue in the midterm elections of 1882. In January 1883, Congress passed a comprehensive civil service bill sponsored by Senator George H. Pendleton of Ohio, providing for the open selection of government employees—to be administered by a Civil Service Commission—and guaranteeing the right of citizens to compete for federal appointment without regard to politics, religion, race, or national origin. Only about 10 percent of the positions in the federal government were covered by the new law, but nearly every president after Chester A. Arthur, who signed the bill into law, broadened its scope. By 1980 more than 90 percent of federal employees were protected by the act.

the federal court system—were created to serve as principal trial courts, which also exercise limited appellate jurisdiction. A local district judge and two Supreme Court justices preside over the circuit courts.

The act established that the Supreme Court would be composed of one chief justice and five associate justices, and any decision rendered would be final. The act also held that the Supreme Court could settle disputes between states and provided for mandatory Supreme Court review of the final judgments of the highest court of any state in cases questioning the validity of a treaty or statute of the United States. In *Cohens* v. *Virginia* (1821), the Supreme Court reaffirmed its right under the Judiciary Act to review all state court judgments in cases arising under the federal Constitution or a law of the United States.

HATCH ACT (1939)

The Hatch Act was a measure enacted by the U.S. Congress aimed at eliminating corrupt practices in national elections. It was sponsored by Senator Carl Hatch of New Mexico following disclosures that officials of the Works Progress Administration were using their positions to win votes for the Democratic Party. The Hatch Act forbade intimidation or bribery of voters and restricted political-campaign activities by federal employees. As amended in 1940, it also severely limited contributions by individuals to political campaigns and spending by campaign committees.

ENDANGERED SPECIES ACT (1973)

The Endangered Species Act is a law that obligates federal and state governments to protect all species threatened with extinction that fall within the borders of the United States and its outlying territories. The U.S. Fish and Wildlife Service (USFWS) of the Department of the Interior and the National Oceanic and Atmospheric Administration (NOAA) of the Department of Commerce are responsible for the conservation and management of fish and wildlife resources and their habitats, including endangered species. The Endangered Species Act allows authorities to determine whether a given species qualifies for endangered or threatened status. It also bars the unauthorized harvest, custody, trade, and transport of endangered plants, animals, and other at-risk organisms and allows for the application of civil and criminal penalties upon those who violate this law. Among other powers, the law gives the federal government the authority to establish cooperative agreements with and award monetary grants to the states to provide protection for at-risk organisms within their borders. In addition, this legislation is aided by a regularly updated endangered species list.

Because the "species" definition extends to subspecies or any distinct population segment capable of interbreeding, threatened subsets of species can also be singled out for protection. In addition, provisions for threatened species—that is, any species expected to become endangered

Bald eagles in Homer, Alaska.

in the future within a substantial portion of its geographic home range—are also included in the law. The Endangered Species Act also promotes the protection of critical habitats (that is, areas designated as essential to the survival of a given species). The Endangered Species Act has been credited with the protection and recovery of several prominent species, such as the bald eagle (*Haliaeetus leucocephalus*), the American alligator (*Alligator mississippiensis*), and the gray wolf (*Canis lupus*).

WAR POWERS ACT (1973)

The War Powers Act, enacted by Congress over the veto of President Richard Nixon, was intended to restrain the president's ability to commit U.S. forces overseas by requiring the executive branch to consult with and report to Congress before involving U.S. forces in foreign hostilities. In passing the legislation, members of Congress believed that they were restoring to Congress some of the constitutional war-making authority that had been effectively surrendered to the president in the Gulf of Tonkin Resolution (1964), which precipitated a massive increase in U.S. involvement in the Vietnam War. Although widely considered a measure for preventing "future Vietnams," the War Powers Act was nonetheless resisted or ignored by subsequent presidents, most of whom regarded it as an unconstitutional usurpation of their executive authority.

DON'T ASK, DON'T TELL (1993)

Don't Ask, Don't Tell (DADT) is the byname for the former official U.S. policy (1993–2011) regarding the service of homosexuals in the military. The term was coined after President Bill Clinton signed a law in 1993 directing that military personnel "don't ask, don't tell, don't pursue, and don't harass." When it went into effect on October 1, 1993, the policy theoretically lifted a ban on homosexual service instituted in World War II, though in effect it continued a statutory ban. In December 2010 both the House of Representatives and the Senate voted to repeal the policy, and President Barack Obama signed the legislation on December 22. The policy officially ended on September 20, 2011.

In the period between winning election as president in November 1992 and his inauguration in January 1993, Clinton announced his intention to seek an end to the U.S. military's long-standing ban on homosexuality. Although the move was popular among many Americans–notably, gay activists who had supported Clinton's campaign–and

Clinton had promised action during the election campaign, few thought he would move on the issue so quickly. The move met with strong opposition even amongst office-holding Democrats. Clinton's declaration put the president at odds with top military leaders and key civilians with oversight responsibilities for the armed forces. However, Clinton managed to gain support for a compromise measure under which homosexual servicemen and servicewomen could remain in the military if they did not openly declare their sexual orientation. Military officers were still overwhelmingly opposed to that approach, fearing that the mere presence of homosexuals in the armed forces would undermine morale.

Under the terms of the law, homosexuals serving in the military were not allowed to talk about their sexual orientation or engage in sexual activity, and in return, commanding officers were not allowed to question service members about their sexual orientation. Although Clinton introduced "Don't Ask, Don't Tell" as a liberalization of existing policy, saying it was a way for gays to serve in the military when they had previously been excluded from doing so, many gay rights activists criticized the policy for forcing military personnel into secrecy and because it had fallen far short of a policy of complete acceptance. The policy did little to change the behaviour of commanders; gay and lesbian soldiers continued to be discharged from service. During the Iraq War, which began in 2003, the policy came under further scrutiny, as many Arab linguists who were gay were discharged by the military.

By the 15-year anniversary of the law in 2008, more than 12,000 officers had been discharged from the military for refusing to hide their homosexuality. When Barack Obama campaigned for the presidency in 2008, he pledged to overturn "Don't Ask, Don't Tell" and to allow gay men and lesbians to serve openly in the military (a stance that was, according to public opinion polls, backed by a large majority of the public). In May 2010, the U.S. House of Representatives and a U.S. Senate panel voted to allow the repeal of "Don't Ask, Don't Tell," pending completion of the Pentagon study and certification by the president, the secretary of defense, and the chairman of the Joint Chiefs of Staff that lifting the ban would not adversely affect military readiness. While the Pentagon review was being carried out, the policy was subject to a lawsuit claiming that it violated the First and Fifth Amendment rights of service members. In September, a federal judge agreed with the plaintiffs, holding that it was unconstitutional, though the ruling did not invalidate the law immediately. Later that month efforts to end "Don't Ask, Don't Tell" stalled in the Senate, when the annual National Defense Authorization Act—which included several contentious bills, including the one that would allow for the law's repeal—was filibustered by Republicans.

In October, "Don't Ask, Don't Tell" was reinstated after a stay was granted as the U.S. Justice Department appealed the injunction. Then on November 30, 2010, the Pentagon released its report of its study on "Don't Ask, Don't Tell," which found that repealing the policy would pose little risk to military effectiveness. Some 70 percent of service members surveyed believed that ending the policy would have mixed, positive, or no impact. However, some 40–60 percent of those in the Marine Corps expressed negative views or concerns about overturning "Don't Ask, Don't Tell." After a continued filibuster of the National Defense Authorization Act, independent U.S. Senator Joe Lieberman and Maine Republican Senator Susan Collins introduced in the U.S. Senate a stand-alone

President Barack Obama signs the repeal of "Don't Ask, Don't Tell," December 22, 2010.

bill that would repeal "Don't Ask, Don't Tell." A similar bill was introduced in the House of Representatives, where it passed 250–174 on December 15. Three days later the measure overcame a Republican filibuster attempt by a vote of 63–33, and the repeal bill was passed later that day 65–31. President Obama praised the vote, releasing a statement that said, "It is time to recognize that sacrifice, valor and integrity are no more defined by sexual orientation than they are by race or gender, religion or creed." Obama signed the bill on December 22. The repeal took effect on September 20, 2011.

PATIENT PROTECTION AND AFFORDABLE CARE ACT (PPACA)

The Patient Protection and Affordable Care Act (PPACA), also known as Obamacare, was signed into law by President Barack Obama in March 2010. The act included provisions that required most individuals to secure health insurance or pay fines (the "individual mandate"), made coverage easier and less costly to obtain, cracked down on abusive insurance practices, and attempted to rein in rising costs of health care. This was widely considered the most far-reaching health care reform act since the passage of Medicare, the U.S. government program guaranteeing health insurance for the elderly, in 1965. A centrepiece of Obama's campaign for the presidency was reform of the U.S. health care system—one that left some 45 million people uninsured. In February 2009, just one month after his inauguration, Obama addressed a joint session of the U.S. Congress, declaring that the time was right for overhauling health care. In June, details began to emerge, with Obama favouring a so-called "public option," a government insurance program that would compete with private businesses. The pharmaceutical industry, said that it would support reform. In August, strident opposition to the efforts began to emerge, as critics decried the reform as "socialized medicine." Among the grievances cited by opponents was that the bill would amount to a government takeover of the health care industry.

Legislation was soon introduced, with Democrats in the House of Representatives favouring more sweeping reform than those in the Senate. Although the Democrats had a filibuster-proof majority (60 votes) in the Senate, aided by independents Joseph Lieberman of Connecticut and Bernie Sanders of Vermont, Lieberman's vote for a public option as well as the votes of conservative Democratic senators could not be assured. On November 7, the House of Representatives passed its version of the health care bill, the Affordable Health Care for America Act, by a slim margin of 220–215. Aiding passage was a compromise on abortion language, because some conservative Democrats, including Bart Stupak of Michigan, threatened to withhold support unless language was added restricting coverage of abortion in any health insurance plan that received federal subsidies. On December 24,

President Barack Obama and Vice President Joe Biden react after the U.S. House of Representatives passed the Patient Protection and Affordable Care Act (PPACA), March 21, 2010.

with all Democrats uniting, the Senate passed its version of the legislation 60–39, which was projected to provide health care to more than 30 million uninsured Americans.

Considerable differences between the Senate and House versions had to be reconciled. In March 2010, just as the historic measure teetered on the brink of defeat, Obama and Democratic leaders mounted a last-ditch campaign followed by legislative maneuvering. Faced with the prospect of defeat of health care reform, the Democrats eventually settled on a strategy whereby the House of Representatives would pass the Senate version of the bill, thereby making it law, and then immediately pass a bill amending ("fixing") the legislation that it would send to the Senate. The Affordable Care Act was signed into law by Obama on March 23, along with the fixes bill on March 30.

By 2016, the last full year of Obama's second term, nearly 20 million formerly uninsured Americans had acquired health care coverage through the new exchanges or through the expansion of Medicaid in participating states, and the rate of increase in premiums for employer-based health insurance was considerably lower than it had been during the decade preceding implementation of the Affordable Care Act. Notwithstanding those successes, Republicans in Congress repeatedly condemned the law throughout Obama's presidency, voting more than 50 times in the House of Representatives to repeal or amend it after the party won control of the chamber in 2010. In 2014 the Republicans also gained a majority in the Senate, and in 2016 Republican Donald J. Trump was elected president of the United States, giving the party control of both the executive and legislative branches of the federal government. Trump, who had long derided Obamacare as an expensive failure, had campaigned on a pledge to replace it with a plan that would provide all Americans with better coverage at lower premiums. Because he had not worked out a detailed alternative, however, he was forced to rely on Republicans in the House to draft a bill.

That task proved to be politically difficult, as it soon became apparent that changes of the sort that Republicans were contemplating—including elimination of the individual mandate, cuts in Medicaid funding, and reductions in advanced tax credits to offset insurance premiums—would disrupt the exchanges and cause several million Americans to lose their health insurance. Divisions between moderate and more-conservative Republicans in the House, and the angry feedback of constituents who now supported some form of the Affordable Care Act, prevented passage of a replacement bill until May 2017. During the next four months, similar divisions doomed several versions of a Senate bill, three of which were dramatically voted down in July; a final version was withdrawn in September. Sharply critical of Congress for having failed to replace the Affordable Care Act, Trump signed an executive order in October that permitted the sale of cheaper health insurance policies with fewer benefits than those that had been required under the law. He also announced that his administration would immediately end federal cost-sharing subsidies that had reduced out-of-pocket expenses for low- and middle-income Americans. In December 2017, Trump signed into law a Republican tax reform package that included a repeal of the individual mandate.

CHAPTER FIVE

WESTERN EXPANSION AND OVERSEAS TERRITORIES

I t took a while for the United States to reach its status as a country made up of 50 states, 16 territories (including Puerto Rico, Guam, and American Samoa), and a federal district (Washington, D.C.). Both Alaska and Hawaii became U.S. states in 1959. The following acts are recognized as key elements in shaping the territories of the United States as they are known today.

MISSOURI COMPROMISE (1820)

The Missouri Compromise was a measure worked out between the North and the South and passed by the U.S. Congress that allowed for admission of Missouri as the 24th state in 1821. It marked the beginning of the prolonged sectional conflict over the extension of slavery that led to the American Civil War.

The territory of Missouri first applied for statehood in 1817, and by early 1819 Congress was considering enabling legislation that would authorize Missouri to frame a state constitution. When Representative James Tallmadge of New York attempted to add an antislavery amendment to that legislation, however, there ensued an ugly and rancorous debate over slavery and the government's right to restrict it. The Tallmadge amendment prohibited the further introduction of slaves into Missouri and provided for emancipation of those already there when they reached age 25. The amendment passed the House of Representatives, controlled by the more populous North, but failed in the Senate, which was equally divided between free and slave states. Congress adjourned without resolving the Missouri question.

When it reconvened in December 1819, Congress was faced with a request for statehood from Maine. The Senate passed a bill allowing Maine to enter the Union as a free state and Missouri to be admitted without restrictions on slavery. Senator Jesse B. Thomas of Illinois then added an amendment that allowed Missouri to become a slave state but banned slavery in the rest of the Louisiana Purchase north of latitude 36°30'. Henry Clay then skillfully led the forces of compromise, and on March 3, 1820, the decisive vote in the House admitted Maine as a free state, Missouri as a slave state, and made free soil all western territories north of Missouri's southern border.

When the Missouri constitutional convention empowered the state legislature to exclude free African Americans and mixed-race persons, however, a new crisis was brought on. Enough northern congressmen objected to the racial provision that Representative Henry Clay was called upon to formulate the Second Missouri Compromise. On March 2, 1821, Congress stipulated that Missouri could not gain admission to the Union until it agreed that the exclusionary clause would never be interpreted in such a way as to abridge the privileges and immunities of U.S. citizens. Missouri so agreed and became the 24th state on August 10, 1821; Maine had been admitted the previous March 15. Although slavery had been a divisive issue in the United States for decades, never before had sectional antagonism been so overt and threatening as it was in the Missouri crisis. Thomas Jefferson described the fear it evoked as "like a firebell in the night." The Missouri Compromise was repealed by the Kansas-Nebraska Act (1854) and was declared unconstitutional in the *Dred Scott* decision of 1857.

FUGITIVE SLAVE ACTS (1793, 1850)

The Fugitive Slave Acts, passed by Congress in 1793 and 1850 (and repealed in 1864), provided for the seizure and return of runaway slaves who escaped from one state into another or into a federal territory. The 1793 law enforced Article IV, Section 2, of the U.S. Constitution in authorizing any federal district judge or circuit court judge, or any state magistrate, to decide finally and without a jury trial the status of an alleged fugitive slave.

The measure met with strong opposition in the Northern states, some of which enacted personal-liberty laws

KANSAS-NEBRASKA ACT (1854)

The Kansas-Nebraska Act changed U.S. national policy concerning the expansion of slavery into the territories by affirming the concept of popular sovereignty over congressional edict. In 1820 the Missouri Compromise had excluded slavery from the Louisiana Purchase (except Missouri) north of the 36°30' parallel. The Kansas-Nebraska Act, sponsored by Democratic Senator Stephen A. Douglas, provided for the territorial organization of Kansas and Nebraska under the principle of popular sovereignty, which had been applied to New Mexico and Utah in the Compromise of 1850.

Written in an effort to arrest the escalating sectional controversy over the extension of slavery, the Kansas-Nebraska Act ironically fanned the flame of national division. It was attacked by free-soil and antislavery factions as a capitulation to the proponents of slavery. Passage of the act was followed by the establishment of the Republican Party as a viable political organization opposed to the expansion of slavery into the territories. In the Kansas Territory, a migration of proslavery and antislavery factions, seeking to win control for their respective institutions, resulted in a period of political chaos and bloodshed.

to hamper the execution of the federal law; these laws provided that fugitives who appealed from an original decision against them were entitled to a jury trial. As early as 1810 individual dissatisfaction with the law of 1793 had taken the form of systematic assistance rendered to slaves escaping from the South to New England or Canada via the Underground Railroad.

The demand from the South for more effective legislation resulted in enactment of a second Fugitive Slave Act in 1850. Under this law, fugitives could not testify on their own behalf, nor were they permitted a trial by jury. Heavy penalties were imposed upon federal marshals who refused to enforce the law or from whom a fugitive escaped; penalties were also imposed on individuals who helped slaves to escape. Finally, under the 1850 act, special commissioners were to have concurrent jurisdiction with the U.S. courts in enforcing the law. The severity of the 1850 measure led to abuses and defeated its purpose. The number of abolitionists increased, the operations of the Underground Railroad became more efficient, and new personal-liberty laws were enacted in many Northern states. These state laws were among the grievances officially referred to by South Carolina in December 1860 as justification for its secession from the Union. Attempts to carry into effect the law of 1850 aroused much bitterness and probably had as much to do with inciting sectional hostility as did the controversy over slavery in the territories.

For some time during the American Civil War, the

Abolitionist Wendell Phillips speaks against the Fugitive Slave Act of 1850 at an antislavery meeting in Boston. The spirit of the abolitionist movement is said to have developed from New England's rigorous moral climate.

Fugitive Slave Acts were considered to still hold in the case of blacks fleeing from masters in border states that were loyal to the Union government. It was not until June 28, 1864, that the acts were repealed.

HOMESTEAD ACT (1862)

The Homestead Act was designed to provide land in the Midwest, Great Plains, and the West to people willing to settle on and cultivate it. The law granted 160 acres (65 hectares) of public land free of charge (except for a small filing fee) to anyone either 21 years of age or head of a family who agreed to live on and cultivate the land for at least five years. The law represented the culmination of the Homestead Movement, which had gradually gathered strength since the 1830s.

From the beginning of the republic, the dominant view of the federal government was that public land should be sold to raise revenue. Seeking to change this view came petitions from western farmers asking that land in the public domain be given without charge to settlers willing to work the land. Up until about 1830 there was little resembling a concerted drive for homestead legislation. But starting in that decade, eastern labourers and reformers of all stripes began to join the farmers in pressing for a homestead act. In 1848 the Free-Soil Party included a plank in the party platform urging distribution of public land to settlers free of charge.

There was significant opposition to the Homestead Movement. Eastern employers did not want workers to have the option of leaving low-paying jobs for a farm in the West, and eastern landowners feared the threat to land values posed by a huge public domain given away to anyone willing to settle on it. Southern slaveholders saw homesteaders as antislavery advocates, so they too blocked homestead legislation.

In 1846, Andrew Johnson of Tennessee emerged as one of the leading spokesmen of the Homestead Movement, but bills introduced in Congress in 1846 and 1852 failed. Only when Southern participation in the federal government ceased in

African American families travel to Kansas as part of the exodus from the South to the West in the 1870s. The Homestead Act of 1862 made owning land in the West an option for everyone.

1861 did homestead legislation become a genuine possibility. The Republican Party, in control of the government, had come out in support of a homestead measure during the 1860 campaign, and on May 20, 1862, President Abraham Lincoln signed the Homestead Act into law. By the turn of the 20th century, more than 80 million acres (32.3 million hectares) had been claimed by a total of 600,000 homestead farmers.

PACIFIC RAILWAY ACTS (1862, 1864)

The Pacific Railway Acts provided federal subsidies in land and loans for the construction of a transcontinental railroad across the United States.

The first Pacific Railway Act (July 1, 1862) authorized the building of the railroad and granted rights of way to the Union Pacific to build westward from Omaha, Nebraska, and to the Central Pacific to build eastward from Sacramento, California. Two years later, the railroads were still hampered in their quest for sufficient capital, and Congress obliged with the second Pacific Railway Act (July 2, 1864), which doubled the size of the land grants and allowed the railroads to sell their own bonds. After the transcontinental railroad was completed in 1869, congressional investigations revealed that some railroad entrepreneurs had illegally profiteered from the two Pacific Railway Acts.

DAWES GENERAL ALLOTMENT ACT (1887)

The Dawes General Allotment Act provided for the distribution of Indian reservation land among individual tribesmembers, with the aim of creating "responsible farmers," from the white person's point of view. It was sponsored in several sessions of Congress by Senator Henry L. Dawes of Massachusetts and finally was enacted in February 1887. Under its terms, the president determined the suitability of the recipients and issued the grants, usually by a formula of 160 acres (65 hectares) to each head of household and 80 acres (32 hectares) to each unmarried adult, with the stipulation that no grantee could alienate his land for 25 years. The American Indians who received land thus became U.S. citizens, subject to federal, state, and local laws. The original supporters of the act were genuinely interested in the welfare of the American Indians, but there were not enough votes in Congress to pass it until it was amended to provide that any land remaining after allotment would be available for public sale. The combined influence of friends of the American Indians and land speculators assured passage of the act.

Under the Dawes Act, Indian life deteriorated in a manner not anticipated by its sponsors. The social structure of the tribe was weakened; many nomadic Indians were unable to adjust to an agricultural existence; others were swindled out of their property; and life on the reservation came to be characterized by disease, filth, poverty, and despondency. The act also provided that any "surplus" land be made available to whites, who by 1932 had acquired two-thirds of the 138 million acres (55.8 million hectares) the American Indians held in 1887.

INDIAN REORGANIZATION ACT (1934)

The Indian Reorganization Act was a measure enacted by the U.S. Congress aimed at decreasing federal control of American Indian affairs and increasing Indian self-government and responsibility. In gratitude for the Indians' services to the country in World War I, Congress in 1924 authorized the Meriam Survey of the state of life on the reservations. The shocking conditions under the regimen established by the Dawes General Allotment Act (1887), as detailed in the Meriam report of 1928, spurred demands for reform.

Many of the Meriam report's recommendations for reform were incorporated into the Indian Reorganization Act. The act curtailed the future allotment of tribal communal lands to individuals and provided for the return of surplus lands to the tribes rather than to homesteaders. It also encouraged written constitutions and charters giving Indians the power to manage their internal affairs. Finally, funds were authorized for the establishment of a revolving credit program for tribal land purchases, educational assistance, and aiding tribal organization.

About 160 tribes or villages adopted written constitutions under the act's provisions. Through the revolving credit fund, many Indians improved their economic position. With the funds for purchase of land, millions of additional acres were added to the reservations. Greatly improved staffs and services were provided in health and education, with more than half of all Indian children in public school by 1950. The act awakened a wider interest in civic affairs, and Indians began asking for the right to vote, which they had been technically granted in 1924.

The act's basic aims were reinforced in the 1960s and 1970s by the further transfer of administrative responsi-

PEACE CORPS ACT (1961)

The Peace Corps Act created the Peace Corps, a government agency of volunteers. The act was passed at the initiation of President John F. Kennedy. Its first director was Kennedy's brother-in-law R. Sargent Shriver. The purpose of the Peace Corps was to assist other countries in their development efforts by providing skilled workers in the fields of education, agriculture, health, trade, technology, and community development. Peace Corps volunteers were assigned to specific projects on the basis of their skills, education, and experience. Once abroad, the volunteer was expected to function for two years as a good neighbour in the host country, to speak its language, and to live on a level comparable to that of the volunteer's counterparts there.

The Peace Corps grew from 900 volunteers serving 16 countries in 1961 to a peak of 15,556 volunteers in 52 countries in 1966. By 1989, budget cuts had reduced the number of volunteers to 5,100, but some increases occurred thereafter, the number of countries served having risen to about 90. The organization's global reach extended in the early 1990s to eastern European countries such as Hungary and Poland (1990), the former Soviet Union (1992), China (1993) and South Africa (1997). By the early 21st century, 136 countries had hosted more than 170,000 Peace Corps volunteers through four decades of service.

bility for reservation services to the Indians themselves, who continued to depend on the federal government to finance those services.

HARE-HAWES-CUTTING ACT (1933)

The Hare-Hawes-Cutting Act was the first law to set a specific date for Philippine independence from the United States. It was passed by Congress as a result of pressure from two sources: American farmers, who, during the Great Depression, feared competition from Filipino sugar and coconut oils; and Filipino leaders, who were eager to run their own government.

The bill was passed by the Senate in December 1932 but was vetoed by President Herbert Hoover. To Hoover's surprise, Congress promptly overrode his veto, and the bill became law on January 17, 1933. The act, however, required approval by the Philippine Senate, and this was not forthcoming. Filipino political leader Manuel Quezon led a campaign against the bill because of provisions in it that allowed the indefinite retention of U.S. military bases in the islands. The Tydings-McDuffie Act, substantially similar to the rejected measure but incorporating minor changes, was accepted by the Philippine Senate in 1934.

BELL TRADE ACT (1946)

The Bell Trade Act was a law that specified the economic conditions governing the emergence of the Republic of the

Philippines from U.S. rule. The act included controversial provisions that tied the Philippine economy to that of the United States.

When the Philippines became independent on July 4, 1946, its economy had been thoroughly devastated by World War II. Payment of war damage claims by the U.S. government and an influx of capital were both desperately needed. The Bell Act set quotas on Philippine exports to the United States, pegged the Philippine peso to the U.S. dollar at a rate of 2:1, and provided for free trade between the two countries for eight years, to be followed by gradual application of tariffs for the next 20 years. Many Filipinos objected to the so-called Parity Amendment, which required an amendment to the Philippine constitution allowing U.S. citizens equal rights with Filipinos in the exploitation of natural resources and operation of public utilities. Nonetheless, some powerful Filipinos involved in these negotiations stood to benefit from the arrangement.

A strong incentive for Philippine acquiescence was the fact that American payment of $800 million in war damage claims was made contingent upon Filipino ratification of the Bell Act. The act remained extremely unpopular in the Philippines and was later superseded by an agreement more favourable to Filipino interests, the Laurel-Langley Agreement, which took effect in 1956.

CHAPTER SIX

FOREIGN RELATIONS, IMMIGRATION, AND NATIONAL SECURITY

W hile the president, as head of state, acts as the representative of the nation to the world, and while certain other departments operating within the executive branch such as the State Department interact directly with foreign officials, Congress has adopted many laws affecting the country's relations with other states.

ALIEN AND SEDITION ACTS (1798)

The Alien and Sedition Acts were four internal security laws passed by the U.S. Congress in 1798 that restricted aliens and curtailed the press in anticipation of an expected war with France. After the XYZ Affair (1797), in which American ministers negotiating a treaty with France to protect U.S. shipping were asked to pay a bribe to the French foreign minister, war between the two countries appeared inevitable. Federalists, aware that French military successes in Europe had been greatly facilitated by political dissidents in invaded countries, sought to prevent such subversion in the United States and adopted the Alien and Sedition Acts as part of a series of military preparedness measures.

The three alien laws, passed in June and July, were aimed at French and Irish immigrants, who were mostly pro-French. These laws raised the waiting period for naturalization from five to 14 years, permitted the detention of subjects of an enemy nation, and authorized the chief executive to expel any alien he considered dangerous. The Sedition Act (July 14) banned the publishing of false or malicious writings against the government and the inciting of opposition to any act of Congress or the president—practices already forbidden in some cases by state libel statutes and the common law but not by federal law. The federal act reduced the oppressiveness of procedures in prosecuting such offenses but provided for federal enforcement.

The acts were mild compared with later wartime security measures in the United States, and they were well received in some places. Jeffersonian Republicans vigorously opposed them, however, as drastic curtailments of liberty in the Virginia and Kentucky Resolutions, which the other state legislatures either ignored or denounced as subversive. Only one alien was deported, but there were 25 prosecutions, resulting in 10 convictions, under the Sedition Act. With the war threat passing and the Republicans winning control of the federal government in 1800, all the Alien and Sedition Acts expired or were repealed during the next two years.

EMBARGO ACT (1807)

The Embargo Act was designed to resist British and French molestation of U.S. merchant ships carrying, or suspected of carrying, war materials and other cargoes to European belligerents during the Napoleonic Wars (c. 1801–1815). At Thomas Jefferson's request, the two houses of Congress considered and passed the act quickly in December 1807. All U.S. ports were closed to export shipping in either U.S. or foreign vessels, and restrictions were placed on imports from Great Britain. The act was a hardship on U.S. farmers as well as on New England and New York mercantile

This etching by Alexander Anderson reflects the hostile reaction to the Embargo Act of 1807.

and maritime interests, especially after being buttressed by harsh enforcement measures adopted in 1808.

Its effects in Europe were not what Jefferson had hoped. French and British dealers in U.S. cotton, for example, were able to raise prices at will while the stock already on hand lasted. The embargo would have had to endure until these inventories were exhausted. Napoleon is said to have justified seizure of U.S. merchant ships on the ground that he was assisting Jefferson in enforcing the act. The Federalist leader Timothy Pickering even alleged that Napoleon himself had inspired the embargo. Confronted by bitter and articulate opposition, Jefferson on March 1, 1809 (two days before the end of his second term), signed the Non-Intercourse Act, permitting U.S. trade with nations other than France and Great Britain.

SMOOT-HAWLEY TARIFF ACT (1930)

The Smoot-Hawley Tariff Act raised import duties to protect American businesses and farmers, adding considerable strain to the international economic climate of the Great Depression. The act took its name from its chief sponsors, Senator Reed Smoot of Utah, chairman of the Senate Finance Committee, and Representative Willis Hawley of Oregon, chairman of the House Ways and Means Committee. It was the last legislation under which the U.S. Congress set actual tariff rates.

The Smoot-Hawley Tariff Act raised the United States' already high tariff rates. In 1922, Congress had enacted the Fordney-McCumber Act, which was among the most punitive protectionist tariffs passed in the country's history, raising the average import tax to some 40 percent. The Fordney-McCumber tariff prompted retaliation from European governments but did little to dampen U.S. prosperity. Throughout the 1920s, however, as European farmers recovered from World War I and their American counterparts faced intense competition and declining prices because of overproduction, U.S. agricultural interests lobbied the federal government for protection against agricultural imports. In his 1928 campaign for the presidency, Republican candidate Herbert Hoover

CHINESE EXCLUSION ACT (1882)

The Chinese Exclusion Act was a law that limited Chinese labour immigration to the United States. By the time of its passage approximately 375,000 Chinese had immigrated to the country, nearly all on the West Coast. The Burlingame Treaty of 1868 provided for unlimited immigration, but denied the Chinese the right of citizenship. During the early 1870s an economic depression and the massing of cheap Chinese labour in West

A market in San Francisco's Chinatown is representative of the strong Chinese presence on the West Coast of the United States, circa 1900.

Coast cities gave rise to competition with American workers, whose demand for higher wages put them at a disadvantage. Fearing civil disorder, Congress in 1879 passed an act restricting Chinese immigration, but President Rutherford B. Hayes vetoed it on the grounds that it violated the Burlingame Treaty. In 1880 the treaty was revised to limit Chinese labour immigration, and on May 6, 1882, Congress passed the Chinese Exclusion Act.

promised to increase tariffs on agricultural goods, but after he took office lobbyists from other economic sectors encouraged him to support a broader increase. Although an increase in tariffs was supported by most Republicans, an effort to raise import duties failed. In response to the stock market crash of 1929, however, protectionism gained strength, and, though the tariff legislation passed only by a narrow margin (44–42) in the Senate, it passed easily in the House of Representatives. Despite a petition from more than 1,000 economists urging him to veto the legislation, President Hoover signed the bill into law on June 17, 1930.

Smoot-Hawley contributed to the early loss of confidence on Wall Street and signaled U.S. isolationism. By raising the average tariff by some 20 percent, it also prompted retaliation from foreign governments, and many overseas banks began to fail. Within two years, some two dozen countries adopted similar duties, making worse an already beleaguered world economy and reducing global trade. U.S. imports from and exports to Europe fell by some two-thirds between 1929 and 1932, while overall global trade declined by similar levels in the four years that the legislation was in effect. In 1934, President Franklin D. Roosevelt signed the Reciprocal Trade Agreements Act, reducing tariff levels and promoting trade liberalization and cooperation with foreign governments.

GULF OF TONKIN RESOLUTION (1964)

The Gulf of Tonkin Resolution was put before the U.S. Congress by President Lyndon Johnson, in reaction to two allegedly unprovoked attacks by North Vietnamese torpedo boats on the destroyers *Maddox* and *C. Turner Joy* of the U.S. Seventh Fleet in the Gulf of Tonkin on August 2 and August 4, 1964, respectively. Its stated purpose was to approve and support the determination of the president, as commander in chief, in taking all necessary measures to repel any armed attack against the forces of the United States and to prevent further aggression. It also declared that the maintenance of international peace and security in Southeast Asia was vital to American interests and world peace.

Both houses of Congress passed the resolution on August 7, the House of Repre-

President Lyndon Johnson signs the Gulf of Tonkin Resolution, giving him power to escalate the Vietnam War after North Vietnamese torpedo boats allegedly attacked U.S. destroyers in the Gulf of Tonkin, August 1964.

sentatives by 414 votes to 0, and the Senate by a vote of 88 to 2. The resolution served as the principal constitutional authorization for the subsequent vast escalation of the United States' military involvement in the Vietnam War. Several years later, as the American public became increasingly disillusioned with the Vietnam War, many members of Congress came to see the resolution as giving the president a blanket power to wage war, and the resolution was repealed in 1970.

In 1995 Vo Nguyen Giap, who had been North Vietnam's military commander during the Vietnam War, acknowledged the August 2 attack on the *Maddox* but denied that the Vietnamese had launched another attack on August 4, as the Johnson administration had claimed at the time.

TREATY ON THE NON-PROLIFERATION OF NUCLEAR WEAPONS (1968)

The Treaty on the Non-proliferation of Nuclear Weapons, also known as the Nuclear Non-proliferation Treaty, was signed in 1968 by the United Kingdom, the United States, the Soviet Union, and 59 other states. The treaty committed the three major signatories, which possessed nuclear weapons, not to assist other states in obtaining or producing them. Ratified by the Senate in 1969, the treaty became effective in March 1970 and was to remain so for a 25-year period. Additional countries later ratified the treaty; as of 2017 three countries (India, Israel, and Pakistan) had refused to sign the treaty, and one country (North Korea) had signed and then withdrawn; these countries are all thought to possess nuclear weapons. In addition, South Sudan, founded in 2011, has not joined. The treaty was extended indefinitely and without conditions in 1995 by a consensus vote of 174 countries at the United Nations headquarters in New York.

The Non-proliferation Treaty was uniquely unequal, as it obliged nonnuclear states to forgo development of nuclear weapons while allowing the established nuclear states to keep theirs. Nevertheless, it was accepted

THE ANTITRUST ACTS (1890,1914)

The Sherman Antitrust Act (1890) was the first legislation enacted by the U.S. Congress to curb concentrations of power that interfere with trade and reduce economic competition. One of the act's main provisions outlawed all restraints on trade between states or with foreign nations. This prohibition applied to formal cartels and on any agreements to fix prices, limit industrial output, share markets, or exclude competition. A second key provision made illegal all attempts to monopolize trade or commerce in the United

(CONTINUED ON THE NEXT PAGE)

(CONTINUED FROM THE PREVIOUS PAGE)

States. These two provisions—the heart of the Sherman Act—were enforceable by the Department of Justice through litigation in the federal courts. Firms found in violation of the act could be ordered dissolved by the courts, and injunctions to prohibit illegal practices could be issued. Violations were punishable by fines and imprisonment. In addition, private parties injured by violations were permitted to sue for triple the amount of damages done them.

For more than a decade after its passage, its only effective use was against trade unions. The first vigorous enforcement of the Sherman Act occurred during the administration of President Theodore Roosevelt (1901–09). In 1914, Congress passed two legislative measures that provided support for the Sherman Act: the Clayton Antitrust Act, which elaborated on the general provisions of the Sherman Act and specified many illegal practices that either contributed to or resulted from monopolization; and the Federal Trade Commission Act, providing the government with an agency that had the power to investigate possible violations of antitrust legislation and issue orders forbidding unfair competition practices.

Whereas the Sherman Act declared only monopoly illegal, the Clayton Act defined as illegal certain business practices that are conducive to the formation of monopolies or that result from them. A notable example is the 1984 breakup of

The 98th and final meeting of the American Telephone & Telegraph Company (AT&T) before the company's divestiture on January 1, 1984.

the American Telephone & Telegraph Company, which left the parent company, AT&T, as a provider of long-distance service and seven regional "Baby Bell" companies providing local telephone service. Many of the original Baby Bell companies have since merged. One of the largest antitrust suits since that time was brought against the Microsoft Corporation. A decision in 1999 found that the company had attempted to create a monopoly position in Internet browser software, but a court-ordered breakup of Microsoft was overturned by an appeals court in 2001.

because, especially at the time of signing, most nonnuclear states had neither the capacity nor the inclination to follow the nuclear path, and they were well aware of the dangers of proliferation for their security. In addition, it was understood in 1968 that, in return for their special status, the nuclear states would help the nonnuclear states in the development of civilian nuclear power (although in the event the distinction between civilian and military nuclear technology was not so straightforward) and also that the nuclear states would make their best efforts to agree on measures of disarmament. In the 2005 Review Conference of the Parties to the Treaty on Nonproliferation of Nuclear Weapons, this inequality was a major complaint against the established nuclear powers.

The treaty has continued to play an important role in sustaining the international norm against proliferation, but it has been challenged by a number of events, including (1) North Korea's withdrawal from the treaty in 2003 and its subsequent acquisition of nuclear weapons, (2) evidence of the progress Iraq made in the 1980s on its nuclear program despite being a signatory to the treaty, and (3) allegations about uranium enrichment facilities in Iran, yet another signatory to the treaty. The credibility of the nonproliferation norm has also been undermined by the ability of India and Pakistan to become declared nuclear powers in 1998 without any serious international penalty—and indeed by India establishing its own special arrangements as part of a bilateral deal with the United States in 2008.

NORTH AMERICAN FREE TRADE AGREEMENT (1992)

The North American Free Trade Agreement (NAFTA) was a treaty designed to gradually eliminate most tariffs and other trade barriers on products and services passing between the United States, Canada, and Mexico. The pact effectively created a free-trade bloc among the three largest countries of North America.

NAFTA was inspired by the success of the European Community in eliminating tariffs in order to stimulate trade among its members. A Canadian-U.S. free-trade agreement was concluded in 1988, and NAFTA basically extended this agreement's provisions to Mexico. NAFTA was negotiated by the administrations of U.S. President George H. W. Bush, Canadian Prime Minister Brian Mulroney, and Mexican President Carlos Salinas de Gortari. Preliminary agreement on the pact was reached in August 1992, and it was signed by the three leaders on December 17, 1992. NAFTA was ratified by the three countries' national legislatures in 1993 and went into effect on January 1, 1994.

NAFTA's main provisions called for the gradual reduction of tariffs, customs duties, and other trade barriers between the three members, with some tariffs being removed immediately and others over periods of as long as 15 years. NAFTA ensured eventual duty-free access for a vast range of manufactured goods and commodities traded between the signatories. Other provisions were designed to give U.S. and Canadian companies greater access to Mexican markets in banking, insurance, advertising, telecommunications, and trucking.

NAFTA produced mixed results. It turned out to be neither the magic bullet that its proponents had envisioned nor the devastating blow that its critics had predicted. Mexico did experience a dramatic increase in its exports, from about $60 billion in 1994 to nearly $400 billion by 2013. The surge in exports was accompanied by an explosion in imports as well, resulting in an influx of better-quality and lower-priced goods for Mexican consumers.

The United States and Canada suffered greatly from several economic recessions, including the Great Recession of 2007–09, overshadowing any beneficial effects that NAFTA could have brought about. Mexico's gross domestic product (GDP) grew at a lower rate compared with that of other Latin American countries such as Brazil and Chile, and its growth in income per person also was not significant, though there was an expansion of the middle class in the post-NAFTA years.

Although NAFTA failed to deliver all that its proponents had promised, it continued to remain in effect. Indeed, in 2004 the Central America Free Trade Agreement (CAFTA) expanded NAFTA to include five Central American countries (El Salvador, Guatemala, Honduras, Costa Rica, and Nicaragua). In the same year, the Dominican Republic joined the group by signing a free trade agreement with the United States, followed by Colombia in 2006, Peru in 2007, and Panama in 2011. According to many experts, the Trans-Pacific Partnership (TPP) that was signed on October 5, 2015, constituted an expansion of NAFTA on a much-larger scale (the United States withdrew from the TPP in 2017).

USA PATRIOT ACT (2001)

The USA PATRIOT Act, formally called the Uniting and Strengthening America by Providing Appropriate Tools Required to Intercept and Obstruct Terrorism Act, was enacted in October 2001 in the wake of the September 11 terrorist attacks. Designed to enable law-enforcement authorities to move more nimbly against terrorist threats, it relaxed legal checks on surveillance and granted the Central Intelligence Agency (CIA) and the Federal Bureau of Investigation (FBI) a freer hand to gather data electronically on citizens and resident foreigners. The legislation, approved by a sweeping majority in Congress, reduced the need for subpoenas, court orders, or warrants for eavesdropping on Internet communications, monitoring financial transactions, and obtaining individuals' electronic records. As part of criminal investigations, law-enforcement and intelligence agencies were authorized to track the Web sites that suspects visited and identify those to whom they sent e-mail. Internet service providers were required to turn over data on customers' Web-surfing habits to authorities on demand.

Many of these provisions were hailed as necessary revisions of surveillance laws to keep increasingly sophisticated and determined terrorists at bay. Civil liberties advocates, however, worried that the PATRIOT Act's easing of judicial oversight and its vague definition of legitimate subjects for electronic surveillance invited abuse and could cast the legal dragnet too wide in the search for incriminating evidence. Most of the law's provisions, however, were made permanent in 2006 by the USA PATRIOT Improvement and Reauthorization Act.

The USA PATRIOT Act paved the way for wider deployment of the controversial FBI program formerly known as Carnivore—in 2001 renamed, less menacingly, DCS 1000—which sifted e-mail for particular addresses or specific text strings (sequences of characters). In December 2001, it was reported that the FBI had developed "Magic Lantern," a so-called Trojan horse program designed to crack encrypted files and e-mails. The program could implant itself surreptitiously in a suspect's computer via an e-mail message and then record keystrokes to obtain the user's passwords. In mid-2002 the Department of Justice (DOJ) announced Operation TIPS (Terrorism Information and Prevention System), a plan to recruit workers such as mail carriers and utility meter readers as informants to spot and report "suspicious activity."

CHAPTER SEVEN

CIVIL LIBERTIES AND SOCIAL WELFARE

While a number of acts passing through the House of Representatives and the U.S. Senate have had to do with structuring the nation, there are plenty of laws that have a direct and visible effect on the daily lives of its citizens. It is important to recognize how the legislative branch has affected human rights over the past two centuries—particularly civil rights and civil liberties, labour standards and worker's rights, women's rights, and social welfare.

VIRGINIA AND KENTUCKY RESOLUTIONS (1798, 1799)

The Virginia and Kentucky Resolutions were passed by the legislatures of Virginia and Kentucky as a protest against the Federalist Alien and Sedition Acts. The resolutions were written by James Madison and Thomas Jefferson (then vice president in the administration of John Adams), but the role of those statesmen remained unknown to the public for almost twenty-five years. Generally, the resolutions argued that because the federal government was the outcome of a compact between the states, any exercise of undelegated authority on its part was invalid, and the states had the right to decide when their powers had been infringed and to determine the mode of redress.

The Virginia and Kentucky Resolutions were primarily protests against the limitations on civil liberties contained in the Alien and Sedition Acts rather than expressions of full-blown constitutional theory. Later references to the resolutions as authority for the theories of nullification and secession were inconsistent with the limited goals sought by Jefferson and Madison in drafting their protests.

INDIAN REMOVAL ACT (1830)

The Indian Removal Act was the first major legislative departure from the U.S. policy of officially respecting the legal and political rights of the American Indians. The act authorized the president to grant Indian tribes unsettled western prairie land in exchange for their desirable territories within state borders (especially in the Southeast), from which the tribes would be removed. The rapid settlement of land east of the Mississippi River made it clear by the mid-1820s that whites would not tolerate the presence of even peaceful Indians there. President Andrew Jackson (1829–37) vigorously promoted this new policy, which became incorporated in the Indian Removal Act of 1830. Although the bill provided only for the negotiation with tribes east of the Mississippi on the basis of payment for their lands, trouble arose when the United States resorted to force to gain the Indians' compliance with its demand that they accept the land exchange and move west.

A number of northern tribes were peacefully resettled in western lands considered undesirable for the white man. The problem lay in the Southeast, where members of what were known as the Five Civilized Tribes (Chickasaw, Choctaw, Seminole, Cherokee, and Creek) refused to trade their cultivated farms for the promise of strange land in the Indian Territory with a so-called permanent title to that land. Many of these Indians had homes, representative

In the foreground, troops can be seen stationed in Tampa Bay, Florida, during the Second Seminole War.

government, children in missionary schools, and trades other than farming. Some 100,000 tribesmen were forced to march westward under U.S. military coercion in the 1830s. Up to 25 percent of the Indians, many in manacles, perished en route. The trek of the Cherokee in 1838–39 became known as the infamous Trail of Tears. Even more reluctant to leave their native lands were the Florida Indians, who fought resettlement for seven years (1835–42) in the second of the Seminole Wars.

The frontier began to be pushed aggressively westward in the years that followed, upsetting the "guaranteed" titles of the displaced tribes and further reducing their relocated holdings.

MARRIED WOMEN'S PROPERTY ACTS (1839)

The Married Women's Property Acts were a series of statutes that gradually expanded the rights of married women to act as independent agents in legal contexts. The English common law concept of coverture, the legal subordination of a married woman to her husband, prevailed in the United States until the middle of the 19th century, when the economic realities of life in North America demanded greater flexibility for women.

Men sometimes could be away from home for months or years at a time; thus, a married woman's ability to maintain a household pivoted upon her freedom

LAND-GRANT COLLEGE ACT (1862)

The Land-Grant College Act, also known as the Morrill Act, provided grants of land to states to finance the establishment of colleges specializing in "agriculture and the mechanic arts." The act granted each state 30,000 acres (12,140 hectares) for each of its congressional seats. Funds from the sale of the land were used by some states to establish new schools. Other states turned the money over to existing state or private colleges to create schools of agriculture and mechanic arts (known as "A&M" colleges). The military training required in the curriculum of all land grant schools led to the establishment of the Reserve Officers Training Corps (ROTC), an educational program for future army, navy, and air force officers. The second Morrill Act (1890) initiated regular appropriations to support land-grant colleges, which came to include 17 predominantly African American colleges and 30 American Indian colleges.

Pictured is Carnegie Library, home to the Black Archives Research Center, on the campus of the Florida Agricultural and Mechanical University in Tallahassee, Florida.

to execute contracts. Furthermore, real estate came to be an important and more abundant trade commodity in the United States. Beginning in 1839 in Mississippi, states began to enact legislation overriding the disabilities associated with coverture. They established the rights of women to enjoy the profits of their labour, to control real and personal property, to be parties to lawsuits and contracts, and to execute wills on their own behalf. Change was slow going; most property rights for women emerged over the course of decades, and, because judges frequently interpreted the statutes stringently, women often had to agitate repeatedly for more expansive and detailed legislation.

SOCIAL SECURITY ACT (1935)

The Social Security Act established a permanent national old-age pension system through employer and employee contributions. The system was later extended to include dependents, the disabled, and other groups. Responding to the economic impact of the Great Depression, 5 million old people in the early 1930s joined nationwide Townsend clubs, promoted by Francis E. Townsend to support his program demanding a $200 monthly pension for everyone over the age of 60. In 1934 President Franklin D. Roosevelt set up a committee on economic security to consider the matter. After studying its recommendations, in 1935 Congress enacted the Social Security Act, providing old-age benefits to be financed by a payroll tax on employers and employees. Railroad employees were covered separately under the Railroad Retirement Act of 1934. The Social Security Act was periodically amended, expanding the types of coverage, bringing progressively more workers into the system, and adjusting both taxes and benefits in an attempt to keep pace with inflation.

President Franklin D. Roosevelt signs the Social Security Act on August 14, 1935.

WAGNER ACT (1935)

The Wagner Act, officially known as the National Labor Relations Act, was the single most important piece of U.S. labour legislation in the 20th century. Following in the footsteps of its precursor, the Norris–La Guardia Act (1932), the Wagner Act was enacted to eliminate employers' interference with the autonomous organization of workers into unions.

Sponsored by Senator Robert F. Wagner, a Democrat from New York, it established the federal government as the regulator and ultimate arbiter of labour relations. It set up a permanent, three-member National Labor Relations Board (NLRB) with the power to protect the rights of most workers (with the notable exception of agricultural and domestic labourers) to organize unions of their own choosing and to encourage collective bargaining. The act prohibited employers from engaging in unfair labour practices, such as setting up a company union and firing or otherwise discriminating against workers who organized or joined unions. Under the Wagner Act, the NLRB was given the power to order elections whereby workers could choose which union they wanted to represent them. The act prohibited employers from refusing to bargain with any such union that had been certified by the NLRB as being the choice of a majority of employees.

FAIR LABOR STANDARDS ACT (1938)

The Fair Labor Standards Act was the first act in the United States prescribing nationwide compulsory federal regulation of wages and hours. It was sponsored by Senator Robert F. Wagner of New York and signed on June 14, 1938, effective October 24. The law, applying to all industries engaged in interstate commerce, established a minimum wage of 25 cents per hour for the first year, to be increased to 40 cents within seven years. No worker was obliged to work, without compensation at overtime rates, more than 44 hours a week during the first year, 42 the second year, and 40 thereafter.

TAFT-HARTLEY ACT (1947)

The Taft-Hartley Act—enacted by Congress over the veto of President Harry S. Truman—amended much of the pro-union Wagner Act of 1935. A variety of factors, including the fear of communist infiltration of labour unions, the tremendous growth in both membership and power of unions, and a series of large-scale strikes, contributed to an anti-union climate in the United States after World War II. Republican majorities in both houses of Congress—the first since 1930—sought to remedy the union abuses seen as permitted under the Wagner Act.

The act, while preserving the rights of labour to organize and to bargain collectively, guaranteed employees the
right not to join unions; permitted union shops only where
state law allowed and where a majority of workers voted
for them; required unions to give 60 days' advance noti-
fication of a strike; authorized 80-day federal injunctions
when a strike threatened to imperil national health or
safety; narrowed the definition of unfair labour practices;
specified unfair union practices; restricted union political
contributions; and required union officers to deny under
oath any communist affiliations.

The Landrum-Griffin Act of 1959 contained provisions that strengthened parts of the Taft-Hartley Act,
which was detested by nearly all elements of organized

WOMEN'S ARMED SERVICES INTEGRATION ACT (1948)

The Women's Armed Services Integration Act
was a law that permitted women to serve as full
members of the U.S. armed forces. During World
War I many women had enlisted as volunteers
in the U.S. military services; they usually served
in clerical roles. When the war ended they were
released from their duties. The same was true

during World War II, when an even greater number of women volunteers served in the armed forces. Although the U.S. Congress in 1943 had given the Women's Army Corps (WAC) full army status during wartime, the WAC law was scheduled to expire on June 30, 1948. In anticipation of this event the leaders of the U.S. Army

Secretary of Defense James Forrestal (*centre*) congratulates (*left to right*) Colonel Geraldine May, Colonel Mary A. Hallaren, Captain Joy Bright Hancock, and Major Julia E. Hamblet after the passage of the Women's Armed Services Integration Act in Washington, D.C.

in 1946 requested that the WACs be made a permanent part of their personnel. Following two years of legislative debate, the bill was passed by Congress in the spring of 1948. Signed into law by President Harry S. Truman on June 12, 1948, as the Women's Armed Services Integration Act, it enabled women to serve as permanent, regular members of not only the army but also the navy, marine corps, and the recently formed air force. The law limited the number of women who could serve in the military to 2 percent of the total forces in each branch.

labour at that time. The act set further union restrictions, barred secondary boycotts, put limits on the right to picket, and allowed greater freedom for individual states to set the terms of labour relations within their borders. The latter provision hampered labour organizing in the South, the least unionized region in the United States.

CIVIL RIGHTS ACT (1964)

The Civil Rights Act was a comprehensive set of legislation intended to end discrimination based on race, colour, religion, or national origin. Title I of the act guaranteed equal voting rights by removing registration requirements and procedures biased against minorities and the underprivileged. Title II prohibited segregation or discrimination in places of public accommodation involved in interstate commerce. The act called for the desegregation of public schools (Title IV), broadened the duties of the Civil Rights Commission (Title V), and assured nondiscrimination in the distribution of funds under federally assisted programs (Title VI). Title VII banned discrimination by trade unions, schools, or employers involved in interstate commerce or doing business with the federal government. The latter section also applied to discrimination on the basis of sex and established a government agency, the Equal Employment Opportunity Commission (EEOC), to enforce these provisions.

The Civil Rights Act was highly controversial at the time of its proposal in 1963. Although President John F.

Kennedy was unable to secure passage of the bill in Congress, a stronger version was eventually passed at the urging of his successor, President Lyndon B. Johnson, who signed the bill into law on July 2, 1964, following one of the longest debates in Senate history. White groups opposed to integration with African Americans responded to the act with a significant backlash that took the form of protests, increased support for pro-segregation candidates, and racial violence. The constitutionality of the act was challenged and upheld by the Supreme Court in the test case *Heart of Atlanta Motel* v. *United States* (1964). The act gave federal law enforcement agencies the power to prevent racial discrimination in employment, voting, and the use of public facilities.

VOTING RIGHTS ACT (1965)

The Voting Rights Act aimed to overcome legal barriers at the state and local levels that prevented African Americans from exercising their right to vote under the Fifteenth Amendment (1870) to the Constitution of the United States. The act significantly widened the franchise and is considered among the most far-reaching pieces of civil rights legislation in U.S. history.

Shortly following the American Civil War (1861–65), the Fifteenth Amendment was ratified, guaranteeing that the right to vote would not be denied "on account of race, color, or previous condition of servitude." Soon afterward the U.S. Congress enacted legislation that made it a federal crime to interfere with an individual's right to vote and that otherwise protected the rights promised to former slaves under both the Fourteenth (1868) and Fifteenth Amendments. In some states of the former Confederacy, African Americans became a majority or near majority of the eligible voting population, and African American candidates ran and were elected to office at all levels of government.

Nevertheless, there was strong opposition to the extension of the franchise to African Americans. Following the end of Reconstruction in 1877, the Supreme Court of the United States limited voting protections under federal legislation, and intimidation and fraud were employed by white leaders to reduce voter registration and turnout among African Americans. As whites came to dominate state legislatures once again, legislation was used to strictly circumscribe the right of African Americans to vote. Poll taxes, literacy tests, grandfather clauses, whites-only primaries, and other measures disproportionately disqualified African Americans from voting. The result was that by the early 20th century nearly all African Americans were disenfranchised.

In the 1950s and early 1960s the U.S. Congress enacted laws to protect the right of African Americans to vote, but such legislation was only partially successful. In 1964 the Civil Rights Act was passed and the Twenty-fourth Amendment, abolishing poll taxes for voting for federal offices, was ratified. The following year, President Lyndon

B. Johnson called for the implementation of comprehensive federal legislation to protect voting rights, suspending the remaining legislation that had been used to thwart voters of colour (i.e. literacy tests). An expansion of the law in the 1970s protected voting rights for non-English-speaking U.S. citizens.

AMERICANS WITH DISABILITIES ACT (1990)

The Americans with Disabilities Act provides civil rights protections to individuals with disabilities and guarantees them equal opportunity in public accommodations, employment, transportation, state and local government services, and telecommunications. Some 43 million disabled people are affected by the law. The public accommodations provisions generally became effective beginning January 26, 1992. They required that necessary changes be made to afford access by persons with disabilities to all public facilities, including restaurants, theatres, day-care centres, parks, institutional buildings, and hotels.

In assessing their difficulties with compliance, many business leaders pointed to the confusion caused by vague language and definitions used in the act. For instance, employers are required to make "reasonable accommodation" for disabled job applicants or employees at the workplace, yet an accommodation need not be made if it would bring "undue hardship" to the employer's business.

Discrimination is prohibited against "qualified" individuals with disabilities. A disabled person need only be able to handle the "essential functions" of a job with or without "reasonable accommodation."

MEGAN'S LAW (1996)

Megan's Law was a statute that required law-enforcement officials to notify local schools, daycare centres, and residents of the presence of convicted sex offenders in their communities. The law was named after Megan Kanka, a seven-year-old New Jersey girl who was brutally raped and murdered in 1994 by a twice-convicted sexual offender who had been living across the street from her home. Similar statutes were passed by many U.S. states in the mid-1990s before its adoption as a federal law in 1996.

Concern about sexually related child abuse, especially pedophilia, became intense during the 1980s. Although the main threat to children continued to come from members of the victim's family, by about 1990 attention had come to be focused on sexual molestation committed by non-family members and strangers, and it was widely believed that offenders in such cases typically attacked many children before they were apprehended. In response, many U.S. states passed stringent sexual predator laws. Under a law passed in Washington state in 1990, for example, convicted sex offenders whom prosecutors considered still dangerous were required to register with local police when they changed residence. New Jersey enacted a law that created a three-tiered classification of offenders based on prosecutors' assessments of how likely it was that the offender would repeat his crime, and it required that police notify local residents of the presence of high-risk offenders. The law was soon imitated in other U.S. states.

NO CHILD LEFT BEHIND ACT (2001)

The No Child Left Behind Act (NCLB) was a U.S. federal law aimed at improving public primary and secondary schools, and thus student performance, via increased accountability for schools, school districts, and states. The act was passed by Congress with bipartisan support in December 2001 and signed into law by President George W. Bush in January 2002.

NCLB introduced significant changes in the curriculum of public primary and secondary schools in the United States and dramatically increased federal regulation of state school systems. Under the law, states were required to administer yearly tests of the reading and mathematics skills of public school students and to demonstrate adequate progress toward raising the scores of all students to a level defined as "proficient" or higher. Teachers were also required to meet higher standards for certification. Schools that failed to meet their goals would be subject to gradually increasing sanctions, eventually including replacement of staff or closure.

Supporters of NCLB cited its initial success in increasing the test scores of minority students, who historically performed at lower levels than white students. Indeed, in the 2000 presidential campaign Bush touted the proposed law as a remedy for what he called "the soft bigotry of low expectations" faced by the children of minorities. Critics, however, complained that the federal government was not providing enough funding to implement the law's requirements and that it had usurped the states' traditional control of education as provided for in the Constitution. Moreover, they charged that the law was actually eroding the quality of education by forcing schools to "teach to the test" while neglecting other parts of the curriculum, such as history, social science, and art.

CONCLUSION

It is often said that since the early 20th century, legislatures have gradually lost power to chief executives in most countries of the world. Certainly, chief executives have assumed an increasingly large role in the making of law through the initiation of legislation that comes before parliaments, assemblies, and congresses; through the exercise of various rule-making functions; and as a result of the growth of different types of delegated legislation. In some jurisdictions, the chief executive has acquired enhanced power to veto bills passed by the legislature. Many governors now use a "line-item veto" to strike particular provisions of a bill passed by the state legislature, thereby effectively remaking the bill instead of simply enacting or killing it. At the federal level, presidents who believe that a certain provision of a bill is unconstitutional or an improper intrusion on executive power have sometimes issued informal "signing statements" to declare their intention to ignore the provision or to apply it only in certain cases.

It is also true that chief executives have come to predominate in the sphere of foreign affairs. By devices such as executive agreements, which are frequently used in place of treaties, chief executives have freed themselves from dependence upon legislative approval as the executive budget and the rise of specialized budgetary agencies in the executive division have threatened the traditional fiscal controls of legislatures. Since the end of the Franklin D. Roosevelt administration in 1945, most U.S. presidents have committed the country's armed forces to major hostilities abroad, but none have asked for or received a formal declaration of war from Congress.

Nevertheless, Congress has sometimes checked executive war making by refusing to pass necessary appropriations bills or by passing legislation to prevent the chief executive from spending already appropriated funds for certain purposes. Congress retains a substantial measure of power with respect to the executive through its oversight of the executive bureaucracy, through its investigative powers, and through its control over legislative programs of foreign aid.

GLOSSARY

ACQUIESCENCE The act of agreeing passively or without objection.

APPORTIONMENT The proportional distribution of members of the U.S. House of Representatives on the basis of each state's population.

APPROPRIATION The act of a legislature authorizing money to be paid from the treasury for a specific use.

BIGOT One who is intolerant of other groups, races, or religions.

BIVOUAC To assemble in an improvised military camp.

BUREAUCRACY The layered and subdivided administration of a government or other complex organization.

DIGNITARY A person who holds high rank.

EMANCIPATION The act of freeing from restraint.

FILIBUSTER To prevent legislation by using obstructive tactics, most commonly by making very long speeches to retain control of the floor.

INCUMBENT Currently holding an official position.

JURISDICTION The extent or territory within which judicial authority may be exercised.

LOBBYIST A person who tries to influence legislation on behalf of a special interest.

MONOPOLIZE To obtain exclusive possession or control; to dominate completely.

PROLIFERATION Rapid growth, as if by producing new parts or offspring.

PROXY An authorized substitute.

RATIFY To confirm by approval or formal sanction.

SECESSION The withdrawal of a state from a larger political body.

SEDITION An act intended to encourage resistance to or incite rebellion against an established government.

SOVEREIGNTY Supreme power or authority, or unconditional autonomy, of a state.

STATUTE A law enacted by a legislature.

TACTICIAN One skilled at employing available means to accomplish an end.

VETO The legally or constitutionally established power to prevent the enactment of measures passed by a legislature.

CHINESE EXCLUSION ACT

Sucheng Chan (ed.), *Entry Denied: Exclusion and the Chinese Community in America, 1882–1943* (1991); Andrew Gyory, *Closing the Gate: Race, Politics, and the Chinese Exclusion Act* (1998); Charles J. McClain, *In Search of Equality: The Chinese Struggle Against Discrimination in Nineteenth-Century America* (1994); Lucy E. Salyer, *Laws Harsh As Tigers: Chinese Immigrants and the Shaping of Modern Immigration Law* (1995).

LIBRARY OF CONGRESS

John Y. Cole, *Jefferson's Legacy: A Brief History of the Library of Congress* (1993), discusses the library's history (1800–1992), collections, and buildings and includes biographical information on 13 librarians of Congress, from John J. Beckley (1802–07) to James H. Billington (1987–2015). John Y. Cole and Jane Aikin (eds.), *Encyclopedia of the Library of Congress: For Congress, the Nation & the World* (2004).

Margaret E. Wagner (ed.), *American Treasures in the Library of Congress: Memory, Reason, Imagination* (1997), gathers 76 of the library's representative American treasures chosen by staff specialists for the library's first permanent public exhibition.

Vincent Virga et al., *Eyes of the Nation: A Visual History of the United States* (1997), is a narrative-in-pictures drawn from the millions of maps, prints, photographs, posters, manuscripts, motion pictures, and other treasures in the special collections of the Library of Congress; it includes seven chapters of historical commentary by the historian Alan Brinkley.

The history and architecture of Library of Congress buildings are discussed in John Y. Cole and Henry Hope Reed(eds.), *The Library of Congress: The Art and Architecture of the Thomas Jefferson Building* (1997); and John Y. Cole, *On These Walls: Inscriptions and Quotations in the Buildings of the Library of Congress* (1995).

NO CHILD LEFT BEHIND (NCLB)

Frederick M. Hess and Michael J. Petrilli, *No Child Left Behind* (2006); Paul E. Peterson and Martin R. West, *No Child Left Behind?: The Politics and Practice of School Accountability* (2003).

TRAIL OF TEARS

Reviews of the causes and effects of Indian removal include David S. Heidler and Jeanne T. Heidler, *Indian Removal* (2007); and Ronald N. Satz, *American Indian Policy in the Jacksonian Era* (2002). Theda Perdue and Michael D. Green, *The Cherokee Nation and the Trail of Tears* (2007), provides a case study of the experiences of a Southeast Indian nation; while Laurence M. Hauptman and L. Gordon McLester III (eds.), *The Oneida Indian Journey: From New York to Wisconsin, 1784–1860* (1999), provides an example from the Northeast nations. Vicki Rozema (ed.), *Voices from the Trail of Tears* (2003), relates eyewitness accounts of the journey, gleaned from newspapers and other sources. Photographs of parts of the trail can be found in David G. Fitzgerald and Duane H. King, *The Cherokee Trail of Tears* (2007).

U.S. CAPITOL BUILDING

Excellent works on the construction and history of the Capitol include Philip Bigler, *Washington in Focus: The Photo History of the Nation's Capital* (1988); Library of Congress, *The Capitol: A Pictorial History of the Capitol and of the Congress*, 9th ed. (1983); Constance McLaughlin Green, *Washington*, 2 vol. (1962–63); A.B. Lakier, *A Russian Looks at America: The Journey of Aleksandr Borisovich Lakier in 1857*, trans. and ed. by Arnold Schrier and Joyce Story (1979; originally published in Russian, 2 vol., 1859); Margaret Leech, *Reveille in Washington, 1860–1865* (1941, reissued 1991); and Fred J. Maroon and Suzy Maroon, *The United States Capitol* (1993).

INDEX